A Positive Approach to the International Economic Order

Part II: Non-Trade Issues

by Alasdair MacBean
Professor of Economics,
University of Lancaster

and
V. N. Balasubramanyam
Senior Lecturer,
University of Lancaster

BRITISH-NORTH AMERICAN COMMITTEE

Sponsored by
British-North American Research Association (UK)
National Planning Assocition (USA)
C.D. Howe Research Institute (Canada)

338.91
P 855
v. 2

ISBN 0-902594-37-0

Published by the British-North American Committee
Printed and bound in the United Kingdom by
Stirling Smith Williams Ltd, 17/21 Great Portland Street, London W1

May 1980

Contents

A POSITIVE APPROACH TO THE INTERNATIONAL ECONOMIC ORDER
PART II: NON-TRADE ISSUES
by Alasdair MacBean and V. N. Balasubramanyam

Statement of the British-North American Committee to Accompany the Report

In 1976 the British-North American Committee asked Alasdair MacBean, Professor of Economics at Lancaster University, to take an objective look at the economic relationship between developed and developing coutries and to see what changes might be of mutual advantage. Part I of his study, published in 1977, dealt with trade and structural adjustment, and was well received.

This second part, in which Professor MacBean is joined by Dr V. N. Balasubramanyam, a colleague at Lancaster, examines three other aspects: aid, external borrowing and foreign direct investment.

We feel that this publication is particularly timely in view of the more uncertain financial conditions for international capital movements and questions about international stability. It is also relevant in the light of the inconclusive outcome of the fifth meeting of the United Nations Conference on Trade and Development (UNCTAD) and the increasing search for other ways of building more satisfactory relationships between developed and developing countries.

While the author's conclusions are their own and not necessarily those of all members of the British-North American Committee, we commend this report for serious study as a further contribution to world economic development in ways which recognise the large commitment of interests among all countries.

Footnotes to the Statement as a whole

Efforts in the United Nations to gain a reasonable degree of common agreement on an all-embracing, voluntary code of conduct for the MNEs are worth pursuing (Ch. 3.E). They could represent a positive attempt to obviate the negative alternative – an increasing web of conflicting national, regional or international rules, regulations and laws which will inevitably discourage the MNEs from fulfilling their potential role as constructive factors in world economic development. A balanced voluntary code would have the practical advantages of flexibility, which is necessary because it is not possible to prescribe specific responses to every industrial and social problem that will arise in a widespread international enterprise, and because MNEs are by no means the homogeneous bodies that many seem to believe they are. By contrast, a mandatory code would pose problems of sovereignty for LDCs and in itself result in individual national legislations which will conflict and confuse. **John H. Hale**

The statement (page 16) 'that improvements in quality probably involve freeing aid from procurement ties and most if not all political strings and commercial objectives' is questionable. The best measure of the quality of aid is its effectiveness in improving the GNP of a country and the general well-being of its people. Strong arguments can be put forward that the most effective use of aid is made by tying grants for infrastructure, education, and health improvement to direct investment by the private sector of the DC through bilateral agreement with the LDC. Such a policy would not exclude open market procurement for some portion of the aid where cost savings were clearly warranted. Suitable bilateral agreements would encourage the rapid transfer of technology by way of private sector investment through the creation of a favourable climate for investment by the private sector of the DC. In this way not only the effectiveness and, thus, quality of the aid will be improved but also its quantity through improved political acceptability to the constituents of the DC. **G. R. Heffernan.**

I have read with interest the comments in Chapter III on transfer of technology. My company has experienced problems in this matter when it has lost control of subsidiaries in developing countries. There is no doubt that it is difficult to persuade oneself that technical skills, particularly in today's advanced disciplines, can readily be made available when there is no ability to control onward "leakage". **A. B. Marshall.**

Although I think there is much useful material in this report, I am obliged to express dissent with the emphasis in two of the fields discussed – official development assistance and private direct foreign investment.

Although the report notes that bilateral aid programs have been dominated by foreign policy and commercial objectives, I do not feel that this goes far enough in characterising situations in which such aid was directly supportive of reactionary and even repressive, if not, in fact, corrupt governments as well. In such situations, aside from the question of how much of the aid actually filtered down to those for whom it was intended, there is also the question of whether the aid was applied in the direction of social progress or merely in support of the existing regime.

Secondly, I believe that the treatment of the role of multinational corporations is much too benign. Whether multinational corporations can operate in the less developed countries to the mutual benefit of both the corporations and the less developed countries, the fact is that some multinationals have economic power greater than some of the less developed countries and operate to their own benefit. They often operate overseas to the detriment of the industries and the workers employed in the industries in their home countries. Furthermore, they are not adequately taxed for their overseas profits, not only placing their competitors in their own countries at an unfair disadvantage but also depriving their own countries of revenues.

Two specific comments: The report states that developing countries would be well advised to subsidize the employment of labour rather than capital (page 91). Our whole experience in the apparel industries in the United States suggests that the consequences of such a policy, if applied to apparel, have been very disruptive of these industries in the United States. Also, the comparison of wages in the United States and South Korea in 1967 (page 77) is out of date. Later data, for 1977, are available, and, although these indicate a narrowing of the gap, there is still a sizable difference. **Jacob Sheinkman**

In his discussion of aid to developing countries, in Chapter I, the author has, I believe, paid inadequate attention to two significant points. Both concern the fundamental issue of productivity. The first is that to the extent that aid is directed to economic development, a basic focus should be on strengthening the capabilities of the developing countries to achieve larger productivity gains – hence improving their potential for faster real growth in average strandards of living and, indirectly, in their longer-term international trade and payments positions. The second is that to the extent that aid is motivated more by welfare considerations, and thus represents an "income redistribution mechanism," it has undoubtedly come under increased constraints during the past decade, and may well come under greater constraints in the decade ahead. The essential reason is that growth, especially productivity growth, has slowed substantially among the developed countries, and appears likely to remain slow in the 1980s. Thus, there has been a reduced real growth margin from which income redistribution can most readily be made. This has already curbed the growth of new government programs for income transfers within most developed countries, and could well lead to cutbacks in the future. In these conditions, increased income redistribution to developing countries is hardly likely to be buoyant. **Arthur J. R. Smith.**

One limitation on increasing technology transfer not referred to in chapter III is the difficulty experienced by people in many developing countries in making use of the technologies. One way of overcoming this is to give a higher priority to assistance from developed countries for improving the quantity and quality of secondary and higher education particularly in the science based subjects. **Sir Mark Turner.**

Members of the Committee Signing the Statement

WILLIAM S. ANDERSON
Chairman of the Board,
NCR Corporation

J. A. ARMSTRONG
Chairman and Chief Executive Officer,
Imperial Oil Limited

A. E. BALLOCH
Old Greenwich, Connecticut

ROBERT, A. BANDEEN
President and Chief Executive Officer,
Canadian National

SIR DONALD BARRON
Group Chairman,
Rowntree Mackintosh Limited

CARL E. BEIGIE
President,
C. D. Howe Research Institute

ROBERT BELGRAVE
Director,
BP Trading Company Limited

JOHN F. BOOKOUT
President and Chief Executive Officer,
Shell Oil Company

T. F. BRADSHAW
President,
Atlantic Richfield Company

JOHN F. BURLINGAME
Vice Chairman of the Board,
General Electric Company

SIR GEORGE BURTON
Chairman, Fisons Limited

SIR CHARLES CARTER
Chairman of Research and Management
Committee,
Policy Studies Institute

J. EDWIN CARTER
Chairman and Chief Executive Officer,
INCO Limited

SILAS S. CATHCART
Chairman and Chief Executive Officer,
Illinois Tool Works

DONALD M. COX
Director and Senior Vice President
Exxon Corporation

JAMES W. DAVANT
Chairman of the Board and Chief Executive
Officer,
Paine Webber Incorporated

DIRK DE BRUYNE
Managing Director,
Royal Dutch/Shell Group of Companies

SIR RICHARD DOBSON
Past President,
B.A.T. Industries Limited

WILLIAM DODGE
Ottawa, Ontario

WILLIAM H. DONALDSON
Dean,
Yale School of Organization and
Management

SIR ALASTAIR DOWN
Chairman,
Burmah Oil Company

GEOFFREY DRAIN
General Secretary,
National Association of Local Government
Officers

JOHN DU CANE
Chairman and Managing Director,
Selection Trust Limited

GERRY EASTWOOD
General Secretary,
Association of Patternmakers and Allied
Craftsmen

HARRY E. EKBLOM
Chairman and Chief Executive Officer,
European American Bancorp

MOSS EVANS
General Secretary,
Transport and General Workers' Union

J. K. FINLAYSON
Vice Chairman,
The Royal Bank of Canada

GLENN FLATEN
First Vice President,
Canadian Federation of Agriculture

ROBERT M. FOWLER
Chairman, Executive Committee.
C. D. Howe Research Institute

MALCOLM GLENN
Executive Vice President,
Reed Holdings Inc.

GEORGE GOYDER
British Secretary, BNAC

*JOHN H. HALE
Executive Vice President,
Alcan Aluminium Limited

THE HON. HENRY HANKEY
Director, Lloyds Bank International Ltd.

AUGUSTIN, S. HART, JR.
Vice Chairman,
Quaker Oats Company

*See footnote to the Statement

*G. R. HEFFERNAN
President,
Co-Steel International Ltd.

HENRY J. HEINZ II
Chairman of the Board,
H. J. Heinz Company

ROBERT HENDERSON
Chairman, Kleinwort Benson Ltd.

JOHN V. JAMES
Chairman of the Board, President and Chief
Executive Officer,
Dresser Industries Inc.

GEORGE S. JOHNSTON
President,
Scudder, Stevens & Clark

JOSEPH D. KEENAN
President,
Union Label and Service Trades Department,
AFL-CIO

TOM KILLEFER
Chairman of the Board and Chief Executive
Officer,
United States Trust Company of New York

CURTIS M. KLAERNER
President and Chief Operating Officer,
Commonwealth Oil Refining Company

H.U.A. LAMBERT
Chairman,
Barclays Bank International Ltd.

HERBERT H. LANK
Honorary Director,
Du Pont Canada Inc.

WILLIAM A. LIFFERS
Vice Chairman,
American Cyanamid Company

RAY W. MACDONALD
Honorary Chairman,
Burroughs Corporation

IAN MacGREGOR
General Partner,
Lazard Freres & Co., New York
Honorary Chairman,
AMAX Inc.

CARGILL MACMILLAN, JR
Senior Vice President,
Cargill Inc.

J. P. MANN
Vice Chairman,
United Biscuits (Holdings) Ltd.

WILLIAM A. MARQUARD
Chairman, President and Chief Executive
Officer,
American Standard Inc.

*A. B. MARSHALL
Chairman,
Bestobell Ltd.

WILLIAM J. McDONOUGH
Chairman, Asset & Liability Management
Committee,
The First National Bank of Chicago

PATRICK M. MEANEY
Group Managing Director,
Thomas Tilling Limited

C. J. MEDBERRY III
Chairman of the Board,
Bank America Corporation & Bank of America
NT & SA

SIR PETER MENZIES
Welwyn, Herts

JOHN MILLER
Vice Chairman,
National Planning Association

*See footnote to the Statement

DEREK F. MITCHELL
Chairman and Chief Executive Officer,
BP Canada Limited

KENNETH D. NADEN
President,
National Council of Farmer Cooperatives

WILLIAM S. OGDEN
Executive Vice President,
The Chase Manhattan Bank, N.A.

PAUL PARE
President and Chief Executive Officer,
Imasco Ltd.

FRANK A. PETITO
Advisory Director,
Morgan Stanley & Co. Incorporated

BROUGHTON PIPKIN
Chairman, BICC Limited

SIR RICHARD POWELL
Hill Samuel Group Ltd.

J. G. PRENTICE
Chairman of the Board,
Canadian Forest Products Ltd.

LOUIS PUTZE
Consultant, Rockwell International

BEN ROBERTS
Professor of Industrial Relations,
London School of Economics

HAROLD B. ROSE
Group Economic Advisor,
Barclays Bank Limited

DAVID SAINSBURY
Director of Finance,
J. Sainsbury Ltd.

WILLIAM SALOMON
Limited Partner,
Salomon Brothers

A. C. I. SAMUEL
Handcross, Sussex.

SIR FRANCIS SANDILANDS
Chairman,
Commercial Union Assurance Company Ltd

HON. MAURICE SAUVE
Executive Vice President, Administrative and
Public Affairs,
Consolidated-Bathurst Inc.

PETER F. SCOTT
President,
Provincial Insurance Company Ltd.

LORD SEEBOHM
A Director,
Finance for Industry

THE EARL OF SELKIRK
President,
Royal Central Asian Society

*JACOB SHEINKMAN
Secretary-Treasurer,
Amalgamated Clothing & Textile Workers'
Union

LORD SHERFIELD
Chairman,
Raytheon Europe International Company

R. MICHAEL SHIELDS
Managing Director,
Associated Newspapers Group Ltd.

GEORGE L. SHINN
Chairman,
The First Boston Corporation

GORDON R. SIMPSON
Chairman,
General Accident Fire and Life Assurance
Corporation Ltd.

SIR ROY SISSON
Chairman,
Smiths Industries Limited

*See footnote to the Statement

*ARTHUR J. R. SMITH
President,
National Planning Association

LAUREN K. SOTH
West Des Moines, Iowa.

E. NORMAN STAUB
Chairman and Chief Executive Officer,
The Northern Trust Company

RALPH I. STRAUS
New York, N.Y.

HAROLD SWEATT
Honorary Chairman of the Board,
Honeywell, Inc.

SIR ROBERT TAYLOR
Deputy Chairman,
Standard Chartered Bank Ltd.

J. C. TURNER
General President,
International Union of Operating Engineers,
AFL-CIO

*SIR MARK TURNER
Chairman,
Rio Tinto-Zinc Corporation Ltd.

WILLIAM I. M. TURNER, JR.
President and Chief Executive Officer,
Consolidated-Bathurst Inc.

JOHN W. TUTHILL
President,
The Salzburg Seminar

W. O. TWAITS
Toronto, Ontario.

MARTHA REDFIELD WALLACE
Director,
The Henry Luce Foundation Inc.

RICHARD C. WARREN
Consultant,
IBM Corporation

W. L. WEARLY
Chairman,
Ingersoll-Rand Company

VISCOUNT WEIR
Chairman and Chief Executive,
The Weir Group Limited

SIR ERNEST WOODROOFE
Former Chairman, Unilever Ltd.

Abbreviations used in this Paper

BSFF	Buffer Stock Financing Facility (of IMF)
CF	Common Fund
CFF	Compensatory Financing Facility (of IMF)
DAC	Development Assistance Committee (of OECD)
DCs	Developed Countries
EFF	Extended Fund Facility (of IMF)
FDI	Foreign Private Direct Investment
GDP	Gross Domestic Product
GNP	Gross National Product
IBRD	International Bank for Reconstruction and Development
IDA	International Development Agency
ILO	International Labour Organisation
IMF	International Monetary Fund
ITA	International Tin Agreement
LDCs	Less Developed Countries
MNE	Multinational Enterprise
MPs	Members of Parliament
MSA	Most Seriously Affected (nations)
NATO	North Atlantic Treaty Organisation
NIEO	New International Economic Order
NOLDC	Non-Oil Less Developed Countries
ODA	Official Development Assistance
OECD	Organisation for Economic Co-operation and Development
OF	Oil Facility (of IMF)
OPEC	Organisation of Petroleum Exporting Countries
SDR	Special Drawing Rights
TF	Trust Fund (of IMF)
UNCTAD	United Nations Conference on Trade and Development
USAID	United States Agency for International Development

Authors' Preface

We are grateful to the British-North American Committee for stimulating and supporting our work on this topic. We owe a special debt to Simon Webley and Sperry Lea for their incisive comments on an earlier draft and editorial suggestions. F. Taylor Ostrander and Carl Beigie made several valuable suggestions which have improved the presentation. We are also grateful to Sir Richard Powell, Sir Ernest Woodroofe and Ian Samuel for their detailed comments. None of these, of course, have any responsibility for any errors which remain or views expressed. These are the sole responsibility of the authors.

January 1980
A. I. MacBean
V. N. Balusubramanyam
University of Lancaster

I. Aid: Long Term Official Flows of Finance to Developing Countries

A. INTRODUCTION

An understanding of the reasons for aid to less developed countries (LDCs) from developed countries (DCs) and of its objectives is crucial in evaluating its past and present results and in prescribing future aid policies. The purpose of this first chapter is to clarify these issues. But before that can be done it is necessary to clarify what we are talking about.

The definition of aid adopted by the Development Assistance Committee (DAC) of the OECD states that, 'The word "aid" refers only to flows which qualify as "official development assistance" (ODA), i.e. grants or loans:

— undertaken by the official sector;

— with promotion of economic development and welfare as main objectives;

— at concessional financial terms (if a loan, at least 25 per cent grant element).'[1]

In addition to financial flows, technical co-operation is also included by DAC as aid. There is also a small flow of private assistance from voluntary charitable agencies (rather less than ten per cent of ODA in amount) to developing countries. This is nearly all in the form of grants and comes within the official definition of aid. Clearly private investment and suppliers' credits are not aid in this definition. Even though they may provide great benefits to recipient countries, private investment is undertaken by the investors to serve their objectives, interpreted broadly to include a host of motives, and is considered in Chapter III. The focus of this chapter, then, is on intergovernmental flows of finance; constraints of space exclude examination of private assistance.

Although official development assistance (ODA) forms the subject matter of this chapter, it should be noted that it is not an altogether satisfactory measure of aid. For instance, the interest and repayment terms on loans differ between donors; this type of assistance should, in principle, be compared in terms of its grant equivalents (see footnote 1). Again, allowance should be made for differences in aid-tying — that is aid tied to procurement in the donor country which reduces the recipient's freedom to buy from the cheapest source and has been shown

---

[1] The grant element consists of the difference between the present value of the loan and the present value of the stream of repayments and interest received by the lender discounted at the market rate of interest as a percent of the loan. The lower the interest actually charged and the longer the period for repayment, the greater the grant element.

to raise the cost of aid goods by 20 per cent or more.[2] The real value of aid is liable to differ substantially from the nominal value. However, in this chapter the DAC definition will be used.

The Rationale for Aid

Aid from richer countries to poorer countries intended to promote their economic development is a very new phenomenon in the history of intergovernmental relations, indeed it is hardly thirty years old. The reasons given for it are many and various, ranging from undiluted self-interest to pure moral obligation. Unsurprisingly, the actual motives of governments are mixed. Such empirical evidence as exists on the distribution of aid among recipient nations suggests that the principal motives of the large donor nations have been political, i.e. the furthering of foreign policy objectives. Criteria such as the degree of poverty have had little influence on the past aid distribution of countries such as the United States, Britain, France and West Germany.[3] The Scandinavian nations and the Netherlands may have been freer of direct political self-interest.

For quite some time aid has attracted little popular support in the OECD nations and this has been reflected in legislatures which have often forced cuts in aid budgets. A recent survey in Britain confirms the lack of enthusiasm for overseas aid in the population at large.[4] A speech last year by J. J. Gilligan, then Administrator of the US Agency for International Development (AID) suggests similar indifference and even hostility to aid among the US public.[5]

From the viewpoint of the developing countries, aid is a moral obligation based partly on what they consider to be their right to compensation for wrongs inflicted upon them by colonial and neo-colonial exploitation in the past and partly on discrimination against them at present by the rich nations who restrict imports and immigrants from LDCs. These last two charges can be supported from examination of many developed nations' policies with respect to import restrictions and immigration policies. As was argued in Part I of this study,

---

[2] Mahbub ul Haq, "Tied Credit: a Quantitative Analysis" in J. Adler and S. Kuznets (eds.)., *Capital Movements and Economic Development* (New York, St. Martin's Press, 1967); J. Bhagwati, "The Tying of Aid," UNCTAD (New Delhi) Conference Proceedings, Vol. IV (New York: United Nations 1968); K. Hay, "The Implications for the Canadian Economy of CIDA's Bilateral Tied Aid Programs" (Economic Council of Canada, 1978).

[3] R. D. McKinlay, "The Aid Relationship: A Foreign Policy Model and Interpretation of the Distributions of Official Bilateral Economic Aid of the U.S., U.K., France and Germany, 1960-70," (Odense Universitet. Samfundsvidenskab, 10 June 1978).

[4] T. S. Bowles, *Survey of Attitudes Towards Overseas Development* (Ministry of Overseas Development, London, 1979).

[5] J. J. Gilligan "Why Foreign Aid," an address to the annual meeting of the International Road Federation (U.S. State Department, Washington D.C., 1978).

agriculture protection, the restrictions of the Multi-Fibres Agreement, tariffs and quotas on industrial exports from LDCs severely limit many LDCs' prospects for improving income and employment by their own efforts.[6] But many LDCs argue that restricting their citizens' freedom to migrate from regions of poverty and unemployment to find work in the better-off nations may impose an even greater obstacle to their rapid self-improvement. The selective immigration policies operated by most industrial nations may mean that scarce resources in the form of skilled and professional manpower tend to be skimmed off from the LDCs, lowering still further their capacity to develop quickly. Common justice, it is argued, requires that policies which inflict injuries on neighbours should be stopped and/or compensation paid. But these arguments, especially on immigration, are not accepted by the industrially developed nations in any case and, apart from specific treaties such as the Treaty of Rome or the General Agreement on Tariffs and Trade, no sovereign nations have shown any willingness to accept responsibility for damage to third parties from the pursuit of their own economic or political advantage.

Spokesmen for aid in the rich countries are often in an embarrassing position. Some arguments they use to persuade their own electorates to support aid can cause offence to the nations intended to receive it. If they point to political gains such as treaties of friendship, support in international fora and positions taken in NATO v. Soviet Bloc disputes, LDCs see their political independence as being undermined by aid. Their resentment may vitiate any political gains to the aid given. Actually, the US Congress has shown itself increasingly sceptical of such claims for aid. As far back as 1973 it initiated legislation to change the US programme of aid into 'New Directions,' as it came to be called. This emphasised economic and social development and rejected the use of development assistance to achieve short-run political or diplomatic aims.

Of late, the mutual interest of both DCs and LDCs in the development of the economies of the LDCs has been stressed as a *raison d'être* for development assistance. Maintenance of supplies of key raw materials and the growth of LDC markets for DC exports are alleged benefits to DCs from giving aid. Conversely, a failure of LDCs to improve their growth performance is said to mean that they will press still more heavily upon the world's scarce supplies of food and energy, raising their prices and spreading inflation to OECD nations. Furthermore, failure to reduce the widening gap between the living standards of most developing countries and the standards of the OECD

---

[6] A. I. MacBean, *A Positive Approach to the International Economic Order, Part I: Trade and Adjustment Assistance* (BNAC, London, Montreal, Washington, November 1978) pp 7-32.

nations is predicted to be likely to lead to great political stresses which could burst into revolution, international terrorism and human repression. These points are all made explicitly in the Gilligan speech.[7]

Each of these three arguments is questionable. Domestic stockpiles, development of mining in OECD nations or under the sea, development of synthetic substitutes, offers of long term contracts for specific key materials, assistance to private investment in exploration and development of minerals in LDCs — these all seem likely to be more direct and cheaper methods of ensuring supplies of raw materials than general aid to developing countries. Indeed the faster their growth the more rapidly will LDCs' own demands for raw materials rise. The same would be true of food and energy. As their incomes rise, demand for more expensive, protein-rich foods will tend to increase competition for food and energy required in its production, processing and distribution. Energy for transport and industry will also rise *pari passu* with their growth.

The suggestion that slow growth in the oil importing LDCs should be a significant factor in the inflation problems of the OECD nations seems like grasping for straws. The responsibility for inflation in the US, Britain and Canada lies mainly with their own governments and populations, with some assistance from the policies of OPEC.[8]

The final argument — that the widening absolute gaps in living standards between rich and most poor nations is likely to prove explosive — is perhaps the most serious one. Certainly the LDCs' potential for inflicting damage upon themselves and others is considerable. The Third World's share of world military expenditure rose from 4 per cent in 1957 to 14 per cent in 1976 (24 per cent if China is included).[9] Of course, there is no convincing evidence that economic development will avoid revolutions and wars. Pakistan and Iran represent two obvious cases where substantial increases in per capita incomes did not ward off, and may even have triggered, revolution and continuing political instability. Yet both were in their time held up as examples of the success of economic co-operation between Western powers and important LDCs.

It is difficult to see how a really convincing case could be made out that general economic aid is usually in the interests of the donor nation. The claimed gains are normally very long run and intangible while the

---

[7] J J. Gilligan, *op. cit.,* pp 4-7.

[8] The causes of inflation are of course the subject of infinite debate but neither of the main schools, monetarist or Keynesian, would seek to place much, if any, responsibility for OECD inflation rates upon the non-oil LDCs' growth or price behaviour. See Carl Beigie, *Inflation is a Social Malady* (BNAC, London, Montreal, Washington, March 1979) for recent commentary.

[9] F. Barnaby, "Arms and the Third World: The Background", *Development Dialogue* No. 1, (Dag Hammarskjold Foundation, Uppsala, Sweden, 1977) pp 18-30.

resource costs are clear and immediate. It is difficult enough to demonstrate that it is even in the interests of the recipients. One of the reasons is that it is quantitatively fairly small and therefore its effects are difficult to measure in macro-economic models with many variables. The reflected benefits upon developed countries are mostly expected to be of a very long-term nature. But over time there are so many imponderables, and so many other factors may change that it may never be possible to show that DCs benefited from providing aid to LDCs. It becomes largely a matter of faith.

In the end we may be thrown back on the simple idea of moral obligation. But there is little evidence that governments recognise any such obligation between nations or that the populations of the rich nations accept any continuing need to restrain their consumption in order to release resources to help poor countries. Within nations most governments accept the need for some redistribution of income and for special measures such as free education and even reverse discrimination to reduce differences in work opportunities and rewards. Most of these policies are accepted by practically all political parties. Differences between them normally focus on the degree of redistribution and methods of implementation, not on the ultimate objective. Why do such beliefs and policies stop at national boundaries?

One answer is that virtually all of the OECD nations are democracies with universal suffrage and *most* of their electorates have family incomes below their national average simply because considerable wealth does remain concentrated in a few hands. The majority have an interest in some redistribution, tempered by recognition of the need to maintain incentives and the possibility that they or their children may move into the upper income groups.

There are tentative moves to take this beyond the nation state within such bodies as the European Community through recognition of the need for regional policies to reduce income disparities within the Community. These have been the *quid pro quo* for the richer countries to achieve other objectives. The institution of a European Parliament and the imminent addition of poorer member nations such as Greece, Spain, Portugal and Turkey may carry the principle further. But we are a long way from a World Government, elected by the masses, which could be subject to similar pressures to help the poor, and the UN is a very ineffective substitute. In the absence of any World Government, the advocates of aid may have to rely on either the altruism of people in the rich nations or some form of bargaining behaviour akin to that of trade unions. To *some* extent the Group of 77 has been attempting the latter.

Altruism does have some power. Evidence of this lies in the substantial sums of money which go through voluntary charitable organisations such as CARE, Christian Aid and Oxfam to LDCs. They also act as a lobby for increased ODA. Self-interest on the part of private companies which export to LDCs or have important investments in them leads them to support some ODA, especially if it is procurement-tied. Unless LDCs can mount some credible threat (and 'commodity power' apart from oil does not seem to provide this)[10] the most effective course for LDCs may be to enlist the help of such groups in more effective propaganda for increased flows of ODA to LDCs.

To sum up:

Attempts to provide sophisticated justifications for aid in terms of benefits to the aid giver are not convincing. Perhaps the simple moral view that rich people have an obligation to help poor people is the only real justification for an aid programme. But such a motive for aid would have implications, illustrated below, for the aid objectives of the rich nations and the aid policies required to achieve them.

B.   OFFICIAL DEVELOPMENT ASSISTANCE (ODA) OBJECTIVES

If it is accepted that there is a moral obligation to provide aid this would imply a long-term aim of ameliorating inequality of income between the richest and poorest people in the world. But if this distinction between people and nations is made it does imply some interventionism on the part of the donor nations. Given the great variety of governments in LDCs, few of them democracies, it is by no means clear that aid given without strings would benefit the poor in these countries. A great deal of aid, probably most in the past, has gone into programmes and projects which have done little or nothing for the most needy. Recognition of past failures to ensure that development brings benefits to the bottom 20 per cent or so of the population has led to major reviews of the aid policies of the World Bank and the DAC member nations. The currently fashionable concern for "basic needs" of the Third World, is the response to recognition of these past failures. It could be interpreted as evidence of at least some humanitarian element in the aid objectives of the rich nations. At least short-term commercial or political gains are much less likely from aid directed towards "basic needs." Such aid is likely to involve much more financing of local costs in smaller scale projects in agriculture, extension work, slum housing improvement, village schools and teachers, vocational training, provision of pure water and sanitation and general health care than has traditionally been the case.

The "basic needs" objective has to be interpreted with some care.

---

[10] See Hugh Corbet, *Raw Materials: Beyond the Rhetoric of Commodity Power* (Trade Policy Research Centre, London, 1975) Part I, p 22; B. Varon and K. Takeuchi, "Developing Countries and Non-fuel Minerals," *Foreign Affairs* (April 1974).

Perhaps the most powerful impact upon poverty would be through creating more job opportunities for poor people. Often this will mean small-scale projects to improve agriculture and the choice of labour intensive technology in many projects in industry or communications, but one must beware of too narrow an approach to the problem. A road may be constructed by many workers with little more than picks and shovels and thus creates far more jobs in its construction than would the use of heavy earth-moving equipment, but would take much longer to complete. If the road were to connect a potentially productive farming area to a large market the delay could mean postponing jobs in agriculture and distribution and the multiplier effects of these peoples' expenditures on the rest of the economy. The capital intensive method could in fact be the approach which creates the greater number of jobs as well as being more economic.

An objective of universal redistribution also runs counter to a previous aid fashion, particularly popular with theorists such as W. W. Rostow and Hollis Chenery in US AID circles in the early 1960s. This is the idea that aid can be concentrated on a few countries with good prospects. These can be rapidly assisted to a point at which they "take off into self sustaining economic growth," after the model of Taiwan and South Korea. Aid can then be switched from them to another group. For most of Africa and South Asia there is no prospect of such rapid catching-up policies. Under any plausible assumptions the absolute gap between their standard of living and that of the OECD nations will have widened enormously by the year 2000. This follows from the simple arithmetic of growth. If LDCs with a per capita income of $200 grow at 6 per cent per annum they would reach $640 in twenty years. Over the same time DCs with $5,000 growing at 3 per cent per annum would reach $9,000. The absolute difference in per capita incomes would almost double. It means that ODA will have to continue for a very long time and be viewed in much the same way as social redistributive policies within nations; but it must aim to create the capacity to generate income, i.e. investment in both physical and human capital, rather than simply act as income support. The general purpose of ODA becomes to help raise the average level of productivity in LDCs in such a way that a fair share of the benefits accrues to the poorer sections of nations in the Third World. The means is by increasing LDCs' physical and human capital (machines and skilled people) and their ability to create these for themselves.

Attempts to direct aid to particular projects or programmes run up against the problem of fungibility. If an LDC government decides to spend say $100m on poverty-alleviation programmes and then receives $50m aid it can reduce its own free-tax-dollar commitment to such programmes by $50m, achieve the same poverty programme and increase, say, upper income housing programmes. The DCs' view that their aid is adding something to the welfare of the very poor may then be largely wrong.

For many LDCs, aid remains crucial to their prospects for development. This is stressed in the *1978 DAC Review* which says:

> However important and successful may be international action in the area of trade, commodities, technology, institutional change and structural change, the deliberate and direct transfer of additional resources to many developing countries will remain vital to their development, at least to the end of the century. Too often this is thought to be an exaggeration, and sometimes even a fallacy. For those who doubt it, it is important to stress certain facts:
> — most of the poorer countries of the world will gain only marginally from improvements in commodity prices and have only limited prospects of diversifying into other sectors for earning foreign exchange. Yet additional foreign exchange is vital to the expansion of their economies, since even with internal redistribution and self-reliant policies, they are too small and too poor to dispense with the need for imports of capital and intermediate goods:
> — international transfers, including aid on the right terms and in support of broad-based development, are indispensable if the poorer countries are to achieve accelerated development and there is to be a chance of eradicating absolute human poverty in the foreseeable future.

The UN Resolution on Official Development Assistance

A resolution of the Seventh Special Session of the UN General Assembly in September 1975 laid down these aims for ODA:

1. "Concessional financial resources to developing countries need to be increased substantially, their terms and conditions ameliorated and their flow made predictable, continuous and increasingly assured so as to facilitate the implementation by developing countries of long-term programmes for economic and social development."
2. It should be untied.
3. More ODA should be channelled through multilateral agencies such as the World Bank, the UN Development Programme and the regional development banks.
4. The terms of aid to the least developed, land-locked and island developing countries should be improved so as to be mainly on a grant basis.[11]

These represent the most common demands made by LDC spokesmen with respect to aid. How far were the developed nations moved to meet them? There is some evidence in what has actually happened since then.

---

[11] UN, *The Seventh Special Session of the General Assembly, 1-16 September 1975: Round-up and Resolution* (New York, 1975) pp 25-26.

Recent Trends

Looked at either from the viewpoint of the recipients or the donor nations ODA seems a relatively small contribution from the rich to the poor nations. In current prices the total net ODA from DAC nations in 1978 was just over $18 billion or $6 per head in the Third World. It averaged only 0.32 per cent of the combined DAC member nations' national incomes. In real terms the flow of ODA has increased little since 1965 (Table 1:1).

Table 1:1
Net Official Development Assistance from DAC
Countries to Developing Countries and Multilateral
Agencies (values in $ billion)

	1965	1970	1975	1976	1977	1978*
	$	$	$	$	$	$
Total ODA Current Prices	5.9	6.8	13.6	13.7	14.7	18.3
ODA Deflator	88	100	190.8	191.4	199.1	232.0†
Total ODA in 1970 Prices	6.7	6.8	7.1	7.2	7.4	7.9
ODA/GNP %						
Total DAC Countries	0.44	0.34	0.36	0.33	0.31	0.32
Canada	—	0.42	0.58	0.46	0.51	0.52
UK	—	0.36	0.37	0.38	0.37	0.40
USA	—	0.31	0.26	0.25	0.22	0.23

Source: DAC, *1978 Review; "Developoment Co-operation"* OECD, Paris, 1978 earlier volumes.
*1978 figures from OECD, Press Release, June, 1979.
†Estimated.   ‡Not available from this source.

Among Canada, the US and the UK, Canada emerges from these figures as more generous than average, but the US, one of the richest nations in the world, appears less than generous, with a small and declining share of GNP allotted to ODA. The UK's ODA, while steady, also falls far short of the UN target. Sweden, with ODA at nearly 1.0 per cent of GNP leads the field of DAC donors, with Norway, Denmark and the Netherlands not far behind.

The other major source of aid to LDCs is from the members of the Organisation of Petrol Exporting Countries (OPEC). Their concessional assistance to LDCs has risen from $1.3 billion in 1973 to about $5.7 billion in 1977 in current prices ($4.7 bilion in 1978). This is just over 2.0 per cent of their combined GNP. Aid from the centrally planned economies is very small. According to the latest OECD Press Release their total resource flow to LDCs amounted to $0.9 billion in 1977 and probably declined to $0.8 billion in 1978, equivalent to about 0.04 per cent of these countries' GNP.

If the major purpose of ODA is to supplement domestic savings and assist the formation of capital, one can gain some perspective from statistics on its contribution to that objective. In 1976 the ratio of ODA receipts to total capital availability was between 7 and 8 per cent. Over 80 per cent was from domestic savings and the rest from private loans and direct investment by foreign companies.[12] Over 90 per cent of the capital available to LDCs stems from their own efforts. Similarly, as a proportion of LDCs ' foreign exchange receipts, ODA was less than 6 per cent in 1976.

Of course ODA has not been spread evenly over LDCs in the way average figures might imply. It has in fact been rather heavily concentrated. India has received a large amount of ODA, but given its enormous size the per capita aid has been less than $3 per annum and has contributed less than 10 per cent of the cost of capital formation. South Vietnam for several years was receiving $25-30 per head, as have Israel and Jordan. These figures illustrate the political motivation underlying most past aid allocations which has been documented in R. J. McKinley's research studies referred to above.

Little if any progress has been made towards the long-standing UN goal of raising ODA to 0.7 per cent of the GNP of the DAC nations. In fact, Table 1:1 shows that for the DAC nations as a group ODA has fallen slightly from the 1975 figure of 0.36 per cent to a 1978 level of 0.32 per cent. The US aid performance has been particularly criticised by LDCs. Under the Marshall Plan the US transferred up to 3 per cent of GNP per annum to aid recovery in Europe and Japan in the late 1940s. But in 1978 US official aid to all LDCs was only 0.23 per cent. The DAC Report for that year also notes that the US failed to meet its aid commitment to the International Development Association (IDA).[13] However, it must be pointed out that despite cuts from Congress, the appropriations for the US aid budget have increased in 1978 and 1979, and this may augur some increase in net disbursements soon. The US, Germany, UK and some other DAC countries have indicated intentions to increase their ODA and Japan has announced that its policy is to double its ODA over the next three years. But deepening recession and recent changes in governments in the UK and in Canada cast a more gloomy light upon the prospects for increased ODA. British ODA in

---

[12] *Prospects of Developing Countries, 1978-85,* (World Bank, November 1977) Table VIII. 1.
[13] DAC *Review 1978, Development Co-operation,* (OECD, Paris, November 1978), p 146.

1980-81 will be at about the same level in money terms as in 1979-80 which implies a substantial decline in real terms as a result of rising prices for aid goods.

Another criticism by LDCs is that ODA is unpredictable. Few donor countries are prepared to commit their resources more than a year in advance. The annual budgeting procedures of most democratic nations make it difficult to change this. What some spokesmen for LDCs would like is something akin to an income tax levied upon DCs so as to ensure a steady and growing revenue available for aid and no subject to discretionary bilateral strings. But this seems far from the thinking of the DAC, OPEC, or even the centrally planned socialist economies.

Aid Terms and Conditions

The financial terms of DAC ODA have improved so that the average grant element for the DAC members' aid as a group is 89 per cent. The cost of taking the final step of putting all bilateral ODA on a grant basis would be small, but would generate a substantial gain in terms of goodwill and would prevent the vexatious problem of LDCs getting into excessive debt, at least from past ODA loans, as opposed to private commercial borrowing — a point developed further in Chapter II.

In recent years there has been some, but not much, progress towards untying aid from source procurement. In 1977 the proportion of all untied DAC ODA was 47 per cent. Canada, at 51 per cent, and UK at 47 per cent are about average, but only 27 per cent of the US ODA is totally untied.[14]

Multilaterial Channelling of Aid

Substantially more ODA now goes through multilateral channels than was the case in the 1960s. The average for 1966-68 was 9 per cent and this rose to 30 per cent in 1976. But the rate of change seems to have slowed, rising only to 31 per cent in 1977. Figures for Canada (40 per cent), UK (30 per cent) and USA (35 per cent) in 1976 show them as average or better on this criterion. Since the recent election, however, the Canadian government has indicated a desire to return to bilateral aid for commercial reasons.

Conditionality

The conditionality of aid is not something which can be measured

---

[14] DAC, *op. cit.*, Table B.4, p 221.

statistically, but it would seem plausible to expect that as aid donors have relaxed their financial terms, they may have imposed more stringent conditions of other kinds. These could be in terms of domestic political conditions, such as maintenance of human rights or they could be economic performance criteria such as improved domestic savings or more rational pricing of agricultural products. Naturally aid recipients would prefer ODA with no strings, but equally naturally the electorates and legislative bodies in the donor nations would like to ensure that aid resources are spent on objectives which they approve. Actually, because of the fungibility of resources it is difficult to do this (see above pp. 7-8, and below pp. 18-19).

Where LDCs would seem to have a legitimate grievance is in conditions which are related to special interests of the donor nation, which may be arbitrary and subject to short-run variation. But where conditions are made public, known in advance, and subject to a broad consensus of international opinion, LDC objections carry little weight. Probably the problem is solved most easily where aid is multilateral and the general principles, objectives and conditions for such aid have been agreed in discussions among both donors and recipient nations. It would, for example, seem inconsistent for any subscribing member of the UN to object to a human rights condition.

"The Least Developed Countries, Land-Locked and Island Economies"

If the peculiar nature of these groups is largely ignored as suggested in Part I, section V (see footnote 6) and this is interpreted as a special plea for more aid to the poorest nations, the DAC nations as a group have moved some way towards meeting that objective. The increase in their aid to low income countries (where income per head is under $400 in 1978 prices) from 1970 to 1977 was 158 per cent but this was still only 57 per cent of DAC's aid commitments in 1977. When OPEC and multilateral commitments are included this rises to 65 per cent.[15]

Approximately 64 per cent of the population of developing countries live in these low income countries so the committed aid per capita figure for them is about average for LDCs in total. But because they have less access to other financial sources, they need a greater than proportionate share of ODA. This is not happening at present either on disbursements or commitments of aid despite some expressions of intent by a few DAC nations.

---

[15] DAC, *1978 Review, op. cit.,* Table VI-4.

C. AID EFFECTIVENESS

The foregoing assessment of recent trends in official development assistance has assumed that ODA can actually serve the purpose of facilitating economic development. The standard argument is that ODA supplies both financial resources and technical assistance which supplement LDCs' own savings and resources of skilled manpower. By doing so it increases their investment and improves their capacity to manage their labour, land and capital more than could have been achieved without the aid.

The main claims of the opponents are: (1) aid replaces rather than supplements domestic savings so that investment is hardly if at all increased by aid; (2) the western equipment and technology introduced are inappropriate to LDCs' factor endowment, being too capital intensive for labour-abundant economies. This causes the capital to output ratio to rise so that investment is less productive; (3) and provides soft options so that governments are able to postpone or avoid making institutional reforms necessary to economic and social progress, and undermines their self-reliance; (4) it promotes the power of central governments through whose hands aid passes and who are encouraged to adopt comprehensive development plans which are naive and absorb too much of a nation's scarce skilled manpower, and thwart entrepreneurial initiative through controls.[16]

Taking these arguments in the same order, it is entirely plausible that an inflow of resources from abroad should lead a nation living near 'the breadline' to take some of the increase in the form of consumption so that investment does not increase by the full amount of the foreign funds. Some increase in consumption may in fact help growth by providing better health and more incentives to output. This would not be bad. But one can think of other cases where ODA breaks a particular bottleneck, such as shortage of foreign exchange, which enables purchase of imported spare parts, components and raw materials essential to the full capacity operation of an economy. That in turn raises income and domestic savings. The supply of foreign resources can, when a country is constrained by balance of payments deficits, enable it to save more. The aid then does not replace domestic

---

[16] K. Griffin, "Foreign Capital, Domestic Savings and Economic Development," *Bulletin,* (Oxford University Institute of Economics and Statistics, May 1970) and P. Bauer, *Dissent on Development* (London, Wiedenfeld and Nicholson, 1971) give respectively left wing and right wing critiques of aid on which this summary is based. See MacBean and Balasubramanyam, *Meeting of the Third World Challenge* (Macmillan, 1978) Chapter 6, for a more extensive review and critique of their views.

savings, nor does it merely supplement them, it complements them.[17]

The empirical evidence put forward by Keith Griffin in support of his case that aid has lowered domestic savings is unconvincing.[18] He was unable to measure aid directly and had to use the current account balance of payments deficit as his proxy for aid. But this includes all capital inflows, short and long-term private and official capital inflows, changes in reserves and 'errors and omissions' in the overall balance of payments account. He finds a negative correlation between his proxy for aid and domestic savings, but even if true the causal relation could run in other ways. A domestic crisis, say, a famine in India, would lead to both a fall in domestic saving and a surge in aid-financed food imports. As Professor Gustave Papaneck comments, "There are no good answers to the question 'What would have happened with less or more foreign resource inflows?' In some circumstances, foreign inflows undoubtedly stimulated savings, so that each dollar of inflows led to more than a dollar of investment, while in other cases they discouraged savings and a dollar of inflows may have led to much less than a dollar of investment. However, as long as both savings and inflows are substantially affected by third factors, the negative correlation between the two found in many studies sheds little or no light on their causal relationship."[19]

Another study by Papaneck, in which a more sophisticated analysis separates the influence of aid from other resource inflows, concludes that aid has been significantly and positively related to growth. But, although based on a larger sample of countries and a finer breakdown of resource inflows his study is also subject to the problems of poor quality data, the statistical problems of cross-sectional analyses and risk of omission of significant explanatory variables.[20]

A recent study of the effects of aid in a particular country, Malawi, by Kathryn Morton of the Overseas Development Institute, concludes that far from inhibiting development, aid was vital to Malawi's economic progress. In particular Malawi's savings, tax receipts as well as investment rose steadily and those self-help efforts were encouraged by the aid policies followed by the major donor, the UK.[21]

---

[17] This is a special and credible case of the "foreign exchange gap" criterion for aid. India, Ceylon, Indonesia and Brazil at various times have been in this position.

[18] Griffin, *op cit*. See also critical comments and his reply in the *Bulletin of Oxford University Institute of Economics and Statistics* (Oxford, May 1971).

[19] G. Papaneck, "The Effect of Aid and Other Resource Transfers on Savings and Growth in the Less Developed Countries," *Economic Journal* (September 1972) p 938.

[20] Papaneck, "Aid, Foreign Private Investment, Savings and Growth in Less Developed Countries," *Journal of Political Economy* (Jan/Feb 1973).

[21] K. Morton, *Aid and Dependence* (London, Croom Helm, 1975).

The second argument, that aid encourages capital intensive production methods, is more generally levelled at private direct investment in industry and possibly wrong there too. Most ODA has gone into social overhead projects. Roads, rail, electrical power and irrigation, education and health have absorbed the lion's share of aid. These projects are necessarily capital intensive and some may well have been uneconomic. Particularly in the early days of aid, project evaluation and implementation were poorly carried out.

The third criticism, that governments are made less self-reliant and encouraged to take soft options is very difficult to evaluate. What would they have done in the absence of ODA? The argument perhaps exaggerates the quantitative importance of ODA. As shown above, for most LDCs aid has been a very small contribution to their resources. Perhaps the most plausible case where it might have done so is in the provision of food aid. The programmes of using US surplus grain and soya in aid under Public Law 480 have been much criticised on the grounds that they depress agricultural prices in LDCs, thus reducing private incentives to produce food and taking the pressure off governments to improve domestic food production. Malaysia and other exporters of vegetable oils blame US 'dumping' of soya oil for lower prices for their exports.

While there may be some truth in the criticism that food aid intended to overcome domestic supply shortages actually aggravated the problem, it is probably much exaggerated. Some food aid was in response to emergencies in South Asia and in the Sahelian countries of Africa; without it deaths and suffering would have been much greater. The more regular PL480 programmes were deliberately designed to have the minimum adverse effects upon local prices. Usually the grains were supplied directly as payment for work on rural development projects designed to aid agricultural production or only released to the market to prevent a rise in food prices as cash payments were made to otherwise unemployed workers now constructing roads, small irrigation works, village schools and similar rural development tasks. A recent study by Hans Singer and P. J. Isenmann finds most of the doubts about food aid misguided and suggests that any disincentive effects have been minor given the scale of food aid in the past.[22]

It might also be argued that aid (including food aid) took the pressure off governments such as those of India and Pakistan to place more emphasis on agricultural development. But it should be remembered that the development literature of the '50s and '60s stressed industrialisation as the key to progress. The example of the

---

[22] Isenmann and Singer, "Food Aid: disincentive effects and policy implications" *Economic Development and Cultural Change* (Vol. 25, No. 2, 1977)

Soviet Union seemed to point the way. Leaders such as Nehru were convinced of the need to foster industry for both economic, geo-political and strategic reasons. It is doubtful if India would have been turned from this path by receiving less aid; withholding aid would simply have increased suffering.

The same is probably true of Professer Bauer's criticism that ODA encouraged comprehensive macro-economic plans and over-centralisation. These were the fashions of the time. Indicative planning was popular among OECD nations at the same time as LDCs were adopting these ideas.

A great deal of it was simply window dressing for the benefit of consortia of donors and to whip up domestic support for governmental policies for development including higher taxes and reduced levels of current consumption.

To sum up, while it is difficult to be categorical the overall effect of aid from DCs on the development of LDCs has probably been positive, but it is far less effective in promoting that end than it could have been. This is hardly surprising given the *melange* of donor objectives which encompass political, commercial and humanitarian motives. At the same time there is a lack of any clear consensus on how to promote real and lasting economic development.

D. CAN AID BE INCREASED AND MADE MORE EFFECTIVE?

From a global viewpoint the questions boil down to — can ODA be increased in grant equivalent terms and can it be made to promote more rapid economic and social development for the majority of people in LDCs? But the quantity and the quality objectives may be inconsistent. Improvements in *quality* probably involve freeing aid from procurement ties, and most, if not all, political strings and commercial objectives. It means channelling more of it through multilateral agencies, relating it to overall performance criteria rather than tying it to individual projects, meeting more local costs, and streamlining and harmonising aid procedures.

But the results of these changes would tend to reduce direct benefits to donor nations and their export industries which result from source tying as well as reducing donor identification with specific projects in particular nations. As a result it is likely to reduce the few incentives to provide ODA. Even were that to happen and ODA actually declined, it is arguable that the improvements in quality would mean that more real development would occur. Before making this case it must be stated that a reduction in ODA is not a *necessary* consequence of such reforms. It depends on public and parliamentary (especially US Congressional) reaction to such a reorientation of aid policies. Such reactions are always hard to judge. Probably the public at large is, in any case, totally unfamiliar with most of the arguments; for them aid to LDCs is probably already considered to be a straight hand-out with no strings attached. Certain interested sections of the public such as members of the UN Association, Christian Aid, the League of American Women Voters and similar reasonably informed groups would probably approve the reforms suggested, but have relatively little influence. In some export oriented industries private companies and labour unions might oppose such a shift in policy, particularly if they feel that they are uncompetitive and unlikely to win aid contracts in a free market. They have often proved to be effective lobbyists. Several countries have already both channelled their ODA through multilateral agencies to a substantial extent and increased their overall contribution to ODA. Canada, Denmark and the Netherlands are examples of where it has been done.[23] If the US were also to move substantially in this direction, it would help to make a substantial difference to both the quantity and quality of aid. Other means of improving the quality of aid are:

- *Grants not Loans*
  It would be sensible to put all bilateral ODA on a grant basis. The average grant element is already close to 90 per cent (with Austria and Japan lagging behind the other nations with a grant element of only 70 per cent); to shift entirely to grants would cost little. This would make clear the humanitarian purpose of ODA and avoid the political embarrassments which arise when countries run into difficulties in meeting repayments. It would also economise on administrative staff in aid agencies.

- *Multilateral versus Bilateral*
  Bilateral aid is often tainted by political and commercial interests which affect its distribution between countries and activities. For instance, French aid has a strong neo-colonial aspect, being concentrated in a group of ex-French territories and French Overseas Departments with a population of around 30 millions. Almost half French bilateral aid goes to Overseas Departments and Territories containing just over 2 million people with a *per capita* income of over $1,000. Most OPEC aid has gone to Moslem countries. American and British aid has been concentrated at times on some relatively small countries such as South Vietnam, Israel and Malta.
  At the present time probably the best available agency for administering aid is the World Bank. No doubt it has many defects and

---

[23] DAC, *Review 1978, op. cit.,* Table A.14 and A.16.

has made some serious blunders, but it probably remains the most effective vehicle for aid. It seems genuinely intent on improving the rate of economic and social development in LDCs. It has the largest collection of experts in the field and it does assess carefully the *ex ante* case for aid and evaluates its effectiveness afterwards. It can afford to do this because there are substantial economies of scale in administering aid. Apart from the US no other donors can approach the massive research and administrative capacity of the World Bank. Because the financial resources it controls, and indirectly influences, are very large, the Bank has more influence over recipients' policies. Provided this influence is wielded objectively and sympathetically it is generally likely to lead to improvements in the economic performance of aid recipients. In general the Bank has gained so much experience that it can do this.

The Bank has been accused of Western, and particularly US domination. Inevitably the nations which provide the resources will wish to see the organisation effectively administered. In the past that has meant that most of the higher ranking staff were drawn from DCs. This is much less true today. However, it is important that the World Bank be seen by LDCs to be objective and this may mean more representatives of LDCs on its governing body and as departmental directors.

Of course it would be wrong to try to shift entirely to multilateral aid at short notice. Among other reasons, the Bank would be swamped. But a steady movement in that direction plus an increase in the use of the Bank as the adviser and co-ordinator on bilateral programmes would improve the efficiency and equity of ODA.

- *Project Versus Programme Aid*

Most of ODA has been provided on a project basis. Generally it has been tied to the supply of the foreign exchange costs of both capital and technical assistance projects approved by the donors. Many years ago Hans Singer pointed out an inherent fallacy in this preoccupation with project evaluation. The point is that most recipients do have some foreign exchange of their own. If they put forward their best, most aid-worthy, projects and these are financed by the donors this means that their own foreign exchange is released to finance armaments, prestigious hotels, international airports or even gold beds for ministers if their tastes happen to run that way. In effect the finance provided by the donor always enables the marginal project to be undertaken. To pretend otherwise is simply to go through a charade for the sake of MPs and Congressmen.

Other objections to project-tied aid are that it may bias the path of development away from that which would be in the best interests of the recipient nation. It may be difficult to refuse if such a gift as a new steel works were offered, but the mill may never have a big enough domestic or export market to operate at full capacity and may have to use imported scrap iron, ore or expensive energy to produce poor quality steel because of lack of good engineers and managers. The value of the resources it absorbs as inputs may exceed the real value of its outputs. Sometimes even if the project itself is inherently a good one the donors' insistence that top civil servants and managers must be diverted to it can handicap other, perhaps more important, activities.

But it is also true that learning how to appraise, choose and implement projects is a necessary and important part of development if, as in most LDCs, governments insist on controlling the process. The aid agencies, and particularly the World Bank, could claim that their emphasis on project evaluation has trained a great many citizens of LDCs in the appropriate techniques and philosophy for selection and implementation of projects. Moreover, they would defend themselves from the charge of exclusive concern with individual projects. The IBRD certainly and probably several major bilateral donors, have always concerned themselves with a country's overall performance and policies. Project evaluation has been carried out against that background.

Much aid has been for complete programmes, such as agricultural reform across a broad front. But within any such programme the success or failure of the individual projects is crucial. Unless one is prepared to leave this to the pricing system and general fiscal incentives, project evaluation is essential. Few LDC governments are prepared to adopt *laissez faire* so that donor agencies are almost bound to be drawn into project evaluation work. The only real alternative is to allocate aid on the basis of general past performance and credible policy intentions, after allowing for differences in poverty. There is something to be said for that, but apart from the technical difficulty of judging past performance and future policies these are politically very sensitive areas. The donors would certainly be accused of using their leverage to interfere with national sovereignty. If aid is to move that way this strengthens the argument for channelling it through multilateral institutions.

E. POSSIBLE NEW SOURCES OF FINANCE?

Revenues from the Oceans

Given the lack of general support for ODA in many of the donor nations it would be a great advantage if some alternative, equitable and steadily growing source of finance to replenish the coffers of the World

Bank (especially IDA) could be found. Richard Cooper has made two attractive suggestions: a royalty on the extraction of oil and other minerals from the seabed in international waters and a tax on fishing in international waters.[24] The incidence of such taxes would fall largely upon the richer nations as it is their mineral companies and fishing fleets which would be taking most out of the sea and the seabed and their citizens who would consume most of the products. In future it seems highly probable that mining the seabed will be an important and growing industry. A comparatively modest rate of royalty would yield little in the near future, perhaps nothing, but might grow to a substantial level in coming years. It would be a small gesture towards recognition of all nations' rights to some share in the rewards from exploitation of such global resources. The tax levels could also be adjusted to serve conservation objectives, particularly important for fishing but this extra objective of limiting fishing in certain areas would affect the tax revenue.

The recent trends in discussions concerning the law of the sea do not hold out much hope for these ideas. The "exclusive economic zone" concept dominates the discussion of fishing rights. This will probably give exclusive control of fishing to coastal nations over a 200 mile zone around their coast lines. The same is likely to be true for oil. It is only for oil outside the 200 mile limit that the negotiating text of the Conference on the Law of the Sea provides for international royalties. But this covers only some 5 to 20 per cent of known off-shore oil reserves and would not generate much revenue even in the relatively far future. For other minerals, estimates in Cooper's article suggest that around 10 million tons of ore could be extracted annually by 1985 and 50 million tons by the year 2000. He suggests that the metal content might be worth $200 million in 1958 and $1 billion by the end of the century. If international corporations were set up and extracted these ores and paid (say) a 50 per cent profits tax this would yield a modest revenue for development purposes. But these Cooper estimates made in 1976 are probably far too optimistic as the difficulties and cost of seabed mining promise to be extraordinarily great.

On the most favourable assumptions Richard Cooper estimates that the total possible revenue for LDCs from taxes on fishing, seabed minerals and oil would be about $4.5 billion by 1985. But on both economic and political grounds this is excessively optimistic. To judge from the difficulties in attaining any agreements in the Law of the Sea Conference it is unlikely that LDCs will in fact gain much from general taxes on such resources in the 1980s.

---

[24] R. M. Cooper, "The Oceans as a Source of Revenue" *North/South Debate* edited by Jagdish N. Bhagwati ed. (MIT Press, 1977), Chapter 4.

Tax on Emigrant Earnings

A further unorthodox proposal, first mooted by Jagdish Bhagwati, is for a tax on emigrants from LDCs who earn relatively high incomes in developed countries.[25] Most such migrants are highly skilled and professional people, many thousands of whom have moved from LDCs to the US, Canada and the UK. Many others have gone to other European nations and to Australasia. More recently even larger numbers have flowed into the OPEC nations to meet their huge demands for skilled and even unskilled workers.

It can be argued that as the individuals and the host countries are reaping the benefits of the nurture, education and training, most of which has been provided by their countries of origin, there should be some recompense to such LDCs. The original suggestion was that the countries in which they worked should levy a special surtax of 10 per cent on their net after-tax income. The proceeds would be distributed to LDCs either directly to their countries of origin or indirectly through a UN fund for development aid.

There would be considerable political difficulties. For example, taxation which discriminated between individuals whose circumstances where otherwise similar would be contrary to laws which forbid discrimination between individuals on the basis of race, religion or national origin in many developed countries. Some emigrants from LDCs are political refugees. They would object to taxation which went directly to their political opponents. But means to overcome these difficulties are not hard to devise. If developing countries imposed the levy and it was agreed by a special UN tax treaty that DCs should collect it and pass it on to a UN fund for disbursement many of the objections would be overcome.[26] The idea clearly has some merit and may be worth pursuing. Already remittances from migrants are a substantial source of foreign exchange to several countries, notably Turkey, India and Pakistan. Professor Bhagwati's estimates for the revenue from such a 10 per cent surtax on the migrants' incomes in the US and Canada alone suggest a figure of about $500 million in 1976. Part of the incidence of the tax would fall on remittances, but given the nature of the family commitments met by remittances they are unlikely to decline much for this reason.

---

[25] See Bhagwati and Partington ed: *Taxing the Brain Drain - a Proposal* (Vol. 1) (North Holland Publishing House, 1976).

[26] It would not then be the DC government which was imposing the tax but LDCs taxing their own nationals living abroad and using the UN and the DC governments as the mechanisms for collection. As the revenues would go to a central fund a given DC would not see itself as taxing, say exiles from a particular country, to directly help that country.

F.   CONCLUSIONS

The argument that increased ODA is in the self-interest of the donor nations is hard to sustain, although exporting firms and other special interests may gain. The claimed gains can usually be achieved more efficiently in other ways. But the principle of equity which is supposed to be the basis of redistribution within nations through taxation, subsidies and social security transfers cannot logically stop at national boundaries. There is a widely accepted moral basis for transfers from the rich to help the improvement of the lot of the poor. For most nations, on the internal distribution analogy, it seems natural to do this through taxation rather than leave it to private charity.

Aid allocation in the past does not appear to have been much influenced by criteria which have much to do with morality, equity or even economic efficiency. International policy objectives and to a lesser extent commercial and cultural ties have dominated past patterns of ODA. If morality (which can embrace both considerations of equity and efficient use of resources since waste in a world of scarcity can be regarded as criminal) is to be the governing principle for ODA, actual donor policies will have to change. Aid would then have to be distributed among recipient nations on the basis of expectations about their ability to use it effectively to promote rising standards of living for the majority of their citizens.

Because of their ability to tie aid to specific sources and projects national aid agencies are constantly subject to pressures from foreign ministries, ministries of commerce and commercial firms. They are therefore unlikely to be able to implement policies of international co-operation uninfluenced by political or commercial objectives. This is an important reason for channelling more of ODA through multilateral rather than bilateral agencies. But as this reduces national control and perceived national self-interest in ODA it runs the risk that ODA will be reduced. The examples of the Netherlands and Scandinavia who both provide more ODA and channel a higher proportion through multilateral agencies argues that the risk may not be great, but of course there are important political and cultural differences between the US, other large OECD countries and small, generally socialist countries. Even if the volume of ODA were to decline it is arguable that the improvement in its quality would more than compensate for any decline in volume. For example, untied aid allows free international tendering, encouraging market forces through competition to lower prices of aid goods, and project and programme selection on economic and social criteria should promote more development per dollar than aid allocations biased by political and commercial considerations.

Novel ways of raising resources for ODA such as internationally levied taxes on fishing and mineral extraction from international waters and the seabed are unlikely to contribute large sums in the 1980s but nevertheless deserve more discussion for the future. A willingness on the part of the industrial nations and their mineral companies to pay generous royalties on seabed mining could speed up the process of gaining international agreement on a start to such mining! But the effect of the tax could be to so reduce the profitability of the operations that seabed mining could be significantly delayed. The Bhagwati-Dellafar proposal for an income tax to be levied on migrants from LDCs to DCs seems a very reasonable way of enabling LDCs to gain some return for their investment in their education and training. It could yield quite substantial sums quite quickly.

II. Debt, Finance and the International Monetary System

A. INTRODUCTION

Developing countries need other types of financing than the long term developmental assistance considered in the previous chapter and that implicit in foreign direct investment, to be discussed in the next chapter. In particular they need to be able to finance balance of payments deficits which are of a temporary nature. The appropriate response to a balance of payments deficit depends upon the nature of its causes. A country faced with a fall in exports or rise in imports that seems likely to be reversed in a relatively short period should not have to adjust to this imbalance by cutting back on domestic demand, employment and growth. The real costs of doing so would be far greater than the costs of liquidating reserve assets and/or borrowing short-term to pay for the excess imports.

If, however, the cause of the balance of payments difficulty is more fundamental — for instance a faster rate of inflation at home than abroad, or a permanent adverse movement of its terms of trade — the deficit nation will have to cut its expenditure on consumption and investment or undertake policies to try to raise its output and exports. But even in these situations where structural change or a slowing of the rate of growth of real income are necessary, the ability to borrow funds to cushion the shock and spread the adjustment process over a longer period can make the human costs more bearable and reduce the risks of political instability.

In principle the problems and their solutions are no different for the industrially developed countries and the LDCs. Both groups have access to their own reserves, official use of quotas with the International Monetary Fund (IMF) borrowing from other Fund facilities, standby credits from the Fund, borrowing from other countries' central banks and commercial borrowing of various types. In practice, however, most LDCs have much greater difficulties in obtaining international credit than do the developed countries. At the same time their needs are probably on the average more urgent than those of the developed nations.

This chapter briefly examines the liquidity requirements of LDCs, the general issue of their debt burden, and its consequences, the relations between the IMF and LDCs and their particular interests in the international monetary system

The Special Liquidity Needs of LDCs

Generally speaking, both the exports and imports of LDCs are more unstable about their trends than are those of the DCs. The problem of export instability is of course widely known and its importance may even be somewhat exaggerated. It is the basis of the demands for the Integrated Programme for the Commodities discussed in Part I of this study. But in fact, as an IMF study pointed out, in many cases imports can be just as unstable.[27] A recent study by Professor Coppock also confirms this for a sample of 80 countries as do calculations of our own shown in the Appendix to this chapter.[28] In recent years the dramatic increases in oil prices have produced enormous changes in the cost of imports for the non-oil LDCs (NOLDCs). Fluctuations in domestic food production and in the price of imported food and fertilisers have been another source of instability in the value of total imports for many LDCs.

Another reason for LDCs' needs for increased liquidity is the inflexibility of their requirements for foreign exchange. Partly this is a function of the need for imported inputs for their industries, partly capital goods for development projects and partly the growing financial costs of servicing past official and commercial debts. The volume of debt and the costs of servicing it have been growing at a sufficient rate over the past 15 to 20 years to cause a certain degree of worry about the proportion of export earnings tied up in this obligation and the risk that some LDCs could be forced to default with severe and widespread effects upon the confidence of commercial lenders. This worry reached near panic level with the sudden surge in commercial debt owed by certain LDCs to a relatively few banks, especially those of the US from whom they borrowed, following the 1973 rise in oil prices. Fears of inability to repay debts have been re-awakened by the further oil price increases in 1979. Whether this really is a crisis, what the risks really are and what remedies are required have become the main focus of debate in the last few years.

B. DEBT

The debt issue, then, can be seen as part of the general question of international monetary reform and of LDCs' special interests in how the international monetary system can meet their needs in a more efficient and equitable manner. But for the poorer LDCs, debt merges with the aid issue. Generally these very poor LDCs (*per capita* income less than $400 at 1978 prices and exchange rates, on the World Bank

---

[27] IMF, *Compensatory Financing of Export Fluctuations: A Report*, (1963) p.17.

[28] J. D. Coppock, *International Trade Instability* (Saxon House 1977) p 125 shows instability indices for exports and imports for 1946-71:

EXPORTS: Mean 10.7, Median 9.4
IMPORTS: Mean 10.6, Median 9.5

definition) have not borrowed much from commercial sources. Their economies and particularly their exports have been too stagnant to give much hope of their being able to repay. Furthermore, they have often had weak and unstable governments. In short, they are poor credit risks. Their debt burden has largely been for ODA received in the past on much harder terms than is common today. Their inability to borrow much in the face of raised oil and other import prices (due to Western inflation) has inevitably meant even slower growth. "For the low income countries, particularly those of South Asia, economic growth was only slightly above the growth of population for the period as a whole (1960-76); it declined in the 1960s and approached zero in 1970-75" according to a recent World Bank report.[29] Their problems and the appropriate solutions differ substantially from those of the middle-income countries such as Brazil, Mexico and Peru, which have borrowed heavily from commercial banks. The two groups of LDCs are thus best considered separately, as in Table 2.1 which shows their contrasting patterns of debt.

Table 2.1

Developing Countries: Medium- and Long-Term Debt Outstanding and Disbursed at Year End 1977. (billion current US dollars)

Capital surplus oil exporters are excluded.

	Low Income LDCs*	Middle Income LDCs†	All LDCs
	$	$	$
To official creditors	39 (37%)	66 (63%)	104 (100%)
To private creditors	10 (6%)	145 (94%)	155 (100%)
Total	49 (19%)	210 (81%)	259 (100%)

Source: World Bank, *World Development Report 1979,* Table 22.
* *Per capita* income of $300 or less in 1977.
† *Per capita* income of more than $300 in 1977.

---

[29] IBRD, *Prospects for Developing Countries 1978-85,* (Washington, November 1977), pp. 5-7. See Chart 2.1 for group comparisons.

Debt Problems of the Poorest LDCs

These countries are generally regarded as poor credit risks and would find it hard to borrow from commercial banks or the private capital market even it they could afford the interest costs. The appropriate remedy for part of their problems would seem to be debt relief and more grant aid.

The arguments for this are that they are very poor, lack the ability to generate fast growth, are currently regarded by DAC as deserving grant aid terms, but in the earlier days of ODA were lent capital at fairly hard terms. The problems they face today are mainly not of their making, e.g. the oil price rises and the ensuing world recession and inflated import prices. Furthermore to adjust their domestic economies to eliminate balance of payments deficits would cause great hardship given their low living standards, slow growth and severe structural problems such as over-dependence on exports of one or two crude materials or agricultural products.

The Group of 77 have sought generalised debt relief for all LDCs but especially for these very poor countries. The costs of their debt service obligations were seen to be severely restricting any possibility of achieving even minimum internationally agreed development targets. Since the 1975 UNCTAD meeting several donor nations have converted past loans into grants, thus cancelling debts of the poorest countries. Canada, Sweden and Switzerland were the first to do this as a contribution to the one billion dollar Special Action Programme agreed to at that UNCTAD meeting in Nairobi. The fact that these actions did not appear to have had any adverse effects upon confidence in private capital markets undermines one of the arguments against debt relief. Other countries such as the United Kingdom have followed suit. In recent years the donor countries have accepted that assistance to the "least developed" countries should be in the form of grants. It would seem only consistent to correct *ex post* the terms of assistance provided in the past to bring them into line with current practice. This appears to have been the view of the previous British Minister for Overseas Development when she spoke in the House of Commons recently of the "logical inconsistency of clawing back debt repayment and interest from countries to which we have already been giving grants for some years."[30] The total amount of interest and principal involved in the UK 'retrospective terms adjustment' (debt relief by another name) was around $1.87 billion. This was the largest debt relief exercise when announced but the annual cost to the UK aid

---

[30] Quoted in Ministry of Overseas Development, *Overseas Development*, No. 71, (London, July 1978).

programme in the form of reduced interest and repayments is only some $124 million.

West Germany has given selective debt cancellations of $2.3 billion and Japan $1.2 billion to some of the least developed countries and several smaller donors have also contributed. In all, the total announced or granted amounts to $6.2 billion giving annual savings on debt servicing costs of $300 million per year for 20 years.

Two provisions in the US 1978 Foreign Assistance Act permit retroactive terms adjustment for past aid loans to the poorest countries. One allows conversion of AID loans to grants, and the other permits local currency from PL 480 Title III sales to be used to repay Title I loans.

A significant advantage of debt relief actions to LDCs is that they release resources which are untied and can therefore be used to buy imports from the cheapest sources. But the total amounts involved at $6.2 billion, while helpful, are as yet a small portion of the total outstanding official debt of the poorer LDCs which was approximately $39 billion in 1977. Of course, how the aid provided by debt relief is distributed among recipient countries may not correspond to some 'ideal criterion' of need and performance. But neither does ODA in general. And, because these debt relief measures have been focussed on the poorer LDCs, the distributional pattern is probably more equitable than past ODA. Since the United States and France have lagged behind other donors, the aid burden implied might seem less equitable, but this is a small matter compared with the present variation between the US and Swedish percentage of GNP allocated to ODA.

Generalised debt relief for all LDCs would be a different matter. Some countries in the upper income group of LDCs have been heavy and sometimes irresponsible borrowers. Others have no financial difficulties in meeting their existing commitments. It can be argued that it would be neither equitable nor efficient to commit a substantial part of current and future ODA to wiping out all official LDC debt. Nevertheless some middle income developing countries may face serious debt servicing problems and these may require special treatment.

Debt Problems of the Middle Income Non-Oil LDCs

By far the greatest part of the LDCs debt has been due to commercial borrowing by a number of middle income developing countries that do not export oil — the so-called Non-oil LDCs (NOLDCs). The middle income countries accounted for 81 per cent of total NOLDCs' debt in 1977 and 94 per cent of private debt. Even among the middle income LDCs debt was concentrated on a few. The nine countries in Table 2.2 accounted for over three-quarters of the commercial debt in 1976. If there is a problem it is concentrated in these few LDCs.

Table 2.2

Total Commercial Bank Claims on Major NOLDC Borrowers (1976)

	All Bank Lenders ($ Billions)	U.S. Bank Lenders	
		($ Billions)	(% of Total)
Brazil	$21.2	$13.9	66%
Mexico	17.8	13.0	73
Peru	2.8	1.9	69
Columbia	1.6	1.3	81
Argentina	3.4	2.3	68
S. Korea	3.9	3.2	82
Philippines	2.6	2.3	88
Taiwan	2.6	2.6	100
Thailand	1.4	0.8	57
Other NOLDCs	17.5	10.4	59
Total NOLDCs	**$74.8**	**$51.7**	**69%**

Source: P. N. Watson: *Debt and the Developing Countries* (Overseas Development Council, Washington DC., Development Paper 136, April 1978), Table 8.

Apparently the share of private indebtedness in total debt in the LDCs rose from 33 per cent in 1967 to 52 per cent in 1976. Between 1973 and 1976 it grew at an average rate of 27 per cent per annum. But this is measured in nominal terms. In fact borrowing, both private and official, grew much more slowly in constant money terms. Indeed it was not much out of step with LDCs' growth in GNP and exports.[31]

So the growth in debt may have had less serious implications than it seemed at first glance. The general inflation reduced the real burden the debt both in terms of amortization and interest costs. For most of the time interest rates have actually been lower than the average world rate of inflation.

---

[31] IBRD, *Prospects for Developing Countries, op.cit.,* p 72.

Countries such as Brazil, Mexico, S. Korea and Taiwan had records of fast growth up to 1972. Their prospects of increasing their exports throughout the '70s and '80s seemed good. For them it would seem to have been quite rational to borrow in order to keep up their high growth rates. The fact that they did so helped a little to reduce the depth of the recession in the mid '70s. The industrial nations should be grateful to them for this.

The fact that their borrowing was largely commercial, at much higher rates than official lending, stems from the fact that insufficient official finance was available at the terms and conditions they wanted. They preferred to pay higher rates of interest to commercial banks than to put themselves in the hands of the IMF whose policy requirements for domestic economic management they regard as too conservative.

Moreover the private banks were eager to lend to them. The banking system from 1974 on was awash with petro-dollars. Reduced business activity in the West pushed the banks into seeking other outlets for their loans. These LDCs with good growth records and stable governments seemed good customers at the time and there may be no reason to doubt that they will continue to be so.

In summary, up to the crisis in Iran in 1978 the problem posed by LDC indebtedness was not as great as had been feared. Inflation significantly reduced the real value of outstanding LDC debt. As Gordon Smith pointed out, "the total present value of debt service payments due over the period 1973-82 on the public debt outstanding at the end of 1972 was reduced nearly 40 per cent by inflation during 1973-76 alone. Primarily because of the debt forgiveness implied by inflation, the ratio of debt outstanding to exports of the non-oil-exporting LDCs rose a mere 8 per cent in 1972-76." In aggregate the problem did not appear severe. More detailed econometric investigations suggested that — "only a limited number of countries are flagged as being in a 'danger zone'", i.e. near a default or debt-rescheduling situation. Comparisons with 1970 suggest only slight deterioration in the general LDC debt service situation.[32] So far only one developing country, Zaire, has been in open default on its loan repayments to banks and it subsequently came nearly up to date.[33]

However, since 1978/79 the situation has changed significantly and there are reasons for concern about the future. *First*, the recovery from recession is proving hesitant and the recession may go deeper as a result of the further "post-Iran" increases in oil prices. *Second*, the

---

[32] G. Smith, "The External Debt Prospects of the Non-oil Exporting Developing Countries", (Overseas Development Council, Washington DC., October 1977), pIX.

[33] Paul N. Watson, *Debt and the Developing Countries* (Overseas Development Council, Washington DC., April 1978), p50.

depressed state of the OECD countries is strengthening the growth of the 'new protectionism' which could reduce LDCs export prospects, especially in manufactures. *Third*, debt service ratios for some countries will rise over 1979-82, and the pace of bank lending to LDCs could slow down, especially if there are worries about overexposure to economic or political risks in some countries. The 1979 revolution in Iran may have added to the assessment of political risk with adverse effects on such lending. *Fourth*, the rise in oil prices in 1979 is expected to push the OPEC surpluses up to $45 billion, which is somewhat less than their 1974 level when expressed in real terms, but is much more concentrated in Saudi Arabia and Kuwait this time. This concentration could add to the risk of instability in the financial markets. *Fifth*, the structure of debt has altered. More of it is short term and private. This increases its cost and the problem of refinancing.[34]

Risks to Banks and LDCs

Some analysts suggest that the risks to the banks are not great. Most lending has been by very powerful US banks. A Federal Reserve Study of the six largest US banks showed that there were only two borrowing countries which each made up as much as 1.5 per cent of these banks' total assets in 1978.[35] A total default by two major LDCs such as Brazil and Mexico simultaneously would have a severe impact, but is extremely unlikely, given their economic strength and desire to maintain their future credit-worthiness. Besides, the reserve position of the non-oil LDCs has significantly improved over the 1973/74 situation. Brazil, with over $10 billion in international reserves, is particularly strong. Despite these grounds for rejecting excessive pessimism there is real cause for concern, particularly if there should be any other shock to confidence.

The major costs of default would fall upon the middle income and some poor LDCs. The most adverse outcome would be a series of situations in which payments fell into arrears and several countries went into default or debt rescheduling in a crisis atmosphere. Such an outcome could cause a further crisis in banking confidence and dry up this important source of finance to LDCs.

Policy Consideration

The appropriate policy to avoid such risks is to identify the countries where a bunching of repayments is likely to occur and which

---

[34] Morgan Guaranty Trust Company, *World Financial Markets* (July 1979), p 8; and Hamish McCrae, Financial Editor, *The Guardian* (10 September 1979) p 17.

[35] Quoted in Watson, *op. cit.*, p 50.

might coincide with a recession or some other circumstances which could affect their ability to meet their obligations. Some of the debt will be official debt arising from past ODA. If the countries belong to the category of very poor LDCs, there is a case for converting the ODA debt to grants as previously argued. For many of the poorer LDCs donors have already done this. But for middle income LDCs that case has to be argued. In so far as past ODA was tied and thus reduced in real value there is a case for adjusting the repayment terms to take account of that. For the rest, a possible course of action is to reschedule the debt on a basis which spreads out the repayments but maintains the present value of the debt. The terms would not be softened, indeed interest rates would have to rise to compensate for delay in repayments so as to have no effect upon the distribution of aid between countries.

For private debt there is a case for a refinancing facility on a multilateral basis. Its function would be to lend to countries on a selective basis on interest terms and conditions which would make the present value of the repayment similar to that of the private loans but spread so as to take care of the bunching problem.[36] Some short-term debt would be rolled over, some would be converted into medium or long-term debt. Probably such a refinancing facility should be administered by the IMF, but it would require additional funds, especially from surplus countries such as some OPEC nations, Japan and West Germany whose surpluses have at times rivalled those of the OPEC nations. Since the interest rates would be quite high there should be little sacrifice involved and a worthwhile general return in helping to ensure uninterrupted trading relationships with LDCs. As the overall costs to the selected LDCs would be no lower (though differently phased) there should be no great attractions to countries to deliberately run into such risks of default.

Since the approach is selective, in terms of picking out only those countries for which anticipatory debt rescheduling or refinancing is required, there is a need to have general agreement on the criteria to be used. This could help to meet the worry some LDCs have that selectivity could mean discrimination on political grounds.

The debt issue has highlighted some weaknesses in the existing international monetary system, but LDCs' worries go much deeper and they have a number of specific interests in its reform.

C. RELATIONSHIPS BETWEEN LDCs AND THE INTERNATIONAL MONETARY FUND

LDCs   have   long   been   critical   of   international   monetary

---

[36] Both of these are suggested by Smith, *op. cit.*

arrangements. They see the main institution, the IMF, as designed without their interests in mind and in its management a creature of the industrial nations. They regard themselves as being treated as second-rate citizens. They claim that their access to credit from the Fund has been less easy than that of industrial nations and subject to more stringent conditions.

Certainly, when the IMF was originally planned at Bretton Woods in 1944 few of the present developing countries outside Latin America existed as independent nations. The architects of the IMF, in so far as they considered the interests of LDCs at all, appeared to assume that they were best served by improved monetary arrangements among the developed nations. No special provisions were made for them, and the Articles of Agreement of the Fund explicitly defined it as an agency for stabilization rather than development, the latter function being assigned to the World Bank. Nevertheless, as the LDCs have emerged as independent nations with special problems, the IMF has evolved a number of facilities specifically designed to meet their stabilization requirements. These include the Compensatory Financing Facility (CFF), the Buffer Stock Financing Facility (BSFF), a review of small quotas in the Fund which increased the sizes of many LDCs' quotas and a softening of IMF attitudes to some exchange practices. More recently these facilities have been further liberalised, and in the wake of the oil crisis new facilities were created: the Extended Fund Facility (EFF), the Oil Facility (OF), the Trust Fund (TF) and Subsidy Account. These were not all exclusively for LDCs, but they did cater for LDCs' special problems and have been heavily used by them. Since 1971 the LDCs have been much more fully represented in the discussions on monetary reform. Nine LDC members were appointed to the Committee of Twenty set up in 1972 to report on all aspects of international monetary reform.

Many, if not most of these developments and reforms in the scope and mechanisms of the IMF have been made in response to the demands of developing countries. But LDCs remain unsatisfied with the service provided to them by the Fund. They have made much less use of the resources of the Fund than have the industrial nations. Although they recognise that progress towards their objectives has been achieved they seek many further reforms. As discussed in some detail below, the present exchange regime of floating rates does not please them. On the whole they would prefer a world of stable exchange rates and of increased liquidity. This last, in their view, should come from a much larger issue of SDRs, biased towards LDCs and gradually replacing gold and the dollar as the basic international monetary asset.

Reasons for LDC discontent:
 (i) Quota Size
    Developing countries have long argued that they have special and
greater needs for access to liquid funds to meet balance of payments
deficits than do developed countries. Because of the economic and
political risks attached to their underdeveloped status LDCs have less
access to commercial finance and this enhances their need to have
access to official finance from the IMF. But the quotas of members of
the IMF are based initially on national income, value of total trade,
and size of monetary reserves, at the time of application for
membership. These criteria, making no distinction between developing
countries and developed countries of course result in developed
countries having much larger quotas. Since quota size is the major
determinant of both access to Fund facilities and of voting power in its
operations, LDCs see this as discriminating against them.
    Probably LDCs, at least the NOLDCs, typically do have a
disproportionately greater need of reserves and access to fund credit
than do the richer nations. Their foreign trade, both exports and
imports, tends to be much more unstable, contributing to more
variability in their balance of payments. Where such variations are
temporary fluctuations about trend, the LDCs need more liquidity to
allow them to maintain their trend rate of growth. Where balance of
payments deficits are signs of fundamental disequilibrium requiring
structural adjustment it has to be recognised that adjustment for them
is more difficult. Their economies are typically more rigid, mobility of
labour is often low, skills and management are scarce. Social and
political institutions may inhibit rapid reallocation of resources.
Political circumstances may prevent severe restrictions being placed on
growth, employment and consumption without risk of serious political
instability. So even where fundamental adjustment is necessary many
LDCs may need medium term finance to ease the adjustment process.
Provided they are willing to make the adjustments and not simply to
use borrowed resources to postpone the inevitable, their case seems
just.
    In fact, their case has been accepted in principle and the Fund has
made several increases in the quotas of small countries and LDCs on
application. In 1966, for example, Greece, Iran, Israel, Mexico,
Philippines, Spain and Venezuela were granted extra increases in
quotas. Other Fund Facilities considered below were created with
these special liquidity requirements of LDCs in mind. But still on the
subject of access to the basic resources of the Fund, LDCs complain
that it is too restricted and subject to excessively conservative
surveillance and interference with their domestic economic policies by
the IMF staff.

(ii) Restrictions on Drawings on Quota and Stand-by Arrangements

The normal policy of the IMF, since quite early in its existence, to the use of its quota by a deficit country is that access to the first 25 per cent is available without question. Usually this is merely the counterpart of gold or convertible currency subscribed by the country to the Fund. Access to the remainder of its quota, the 'credit tranches', is progressively more difficult. On the first of the credit tranches the Fund's policy is normally liberal and requires only that the member is making reasonable efforts to solve its balance of payments problems. The conditions become more stringent for the further credit tranches and the member is required to demonstrate convincingly that the policies it is following or intending are adequate to the task.

Since 1952 most ordinary drawings on the IMF have been made under stand-by arrangements, which give the member an assured line of credit for a fixed period, normally twelve months. Before the stand-by arrangement is concluded the member has to come to an agreement with the Fund about the policies it intends to follow. These are embodied in a 'letter of intent' setting out the country's economic objectives and policies. The standby arrangement guarantees that the first credit tranche can be used without further conditions, but additional credit requires evidence of performance. Usually this implies monetary stringency or other approved balance of payments adjustment efforts.

Many LDCs have made use of stand-by arrangements and have no doubt benefited from the credit and the technical advice from the Fund. Usually they have also found that the arrangement with the Fund increases access to assistance from other official and commercial sources. But a general complaint voiced by LDC spokesmen is that the Fund has not really appreciated their special circumstances, in particular the very high priority they must give to development. They claim that LDCs which have been obliged to make use of Fund credit have been forced to adopt IMF recommendations to deflate their domestic economy and liberalise their trade by reducing tariffs, quotas, import licensing and multiple exchange rates. These policies have, in their view, caused excessive hardship and damaged social and economic development. Other LDCs have viewed Fund recommendations with such dismay that they have avoided using Fund facilities or at least kept their use of credit below the levels at which they would have to accept IMF staff policy recommendations.

It is true that LDCs have made much less use of Fund resources than OECD nations, particularly pre-1973. This was not because of less balance of payment problems, and therefore it seems likely that it was at least in part due to an aversion to IMF discipline. LDC politicians are not alone in protesting about the draconic measures allegedly imposed upon them by Fund advisers. British and Italian politicians have made similar accusations. But all such statements should be treated with care. It is not unusual for politicians to seek a foreign scapegoat for the medicine necessary to counteract their own previous weaknesses or errors of judgement. Policies to control inflation which governments know are essential are also often painful and it is useful to be able to blame the 'hatchet men' of the Fund for unemployment, reduced food subsidies, lowered real incomes, and other such effects of reduced government expenditures, or increased taxation.

But does the Fund stand justly accused of insensitivity to the needs of LDCs in adjusting to their balance of payments difficulties? This is an area of controversy where judgement depends upon views on the principal causes of inflation in LDCs and on the proper role of the Fund.[37] The IMF's charter lays down that its major concern is with balance of payments problems. Its loans are short-term and it is not required to concern itself with long-term lending and development. These are explicitly the tasks of its sister institution, the World Bank. They occupy adjacent buildings in Washington and often work closely together. This kinship may meet in part the objection that the IMF is not itself development orientated.

As for the analysis of inflation in LDCs, this breaks into two broad schools. One regards inflation as largely the result of excess demand generated by deficit spending by governments and over-expansion of the money supply. The other school seeks the explanation in underlying stuctural conditions which make it difficult, if not impossible, to achieve development without causing inflation. Immobility of factors of production, absentee landlords, backward agriculture, downward rigidity of prices and ratchet effects of balance of payments surpluses and deficits, and difficulties in taxing politically entrenched sections of the community — these are the major examples of structural rigidities adduced in support of this theory. Structuralist inflation theories have attracted much support in many LDCs, especially in Latin America. Naturally they lead to very critical attitudes towards an IMF which generally takes a more traditional Monetarist view of causes of inflation. But even most structuralists accept the need to control high rates of inflation and in practice the only weapons available to government which can make any impact within an acceptable time scale are deflationary policies with wage and price controls as a possibly helpful supplement. The Fund has

---

[37] This has been made clearer by the adoption in January 1976 of the Second Amendment of the IMF Articles of Agreement which deals with surveillance by the Fund.

generally taken the view that stability of prices was in any case an important precondition for sustained development. The empirical evidence so far published on the issue of whether inflation promotes or inhibits development and *vice-versa* is quite inconclusive. Some countries with high inflation, such as Brazil, have grown fast for decades; others with relatively stable prices such as Malaysia or South Korea have grown as fast for just as long.

The other frequent policy recommendation — trade liberalisation — gains formidable support from two major independent studies of trade policies and development.[38] Both show that policies of import-substituting industrialisation behind high protection have inhibited development, while more realistic exchange rates and export promotion have led to fast growth. In general the trade policies recommended by the Fund have been the correct strategies for growth as well as stability.

No doubt the Fund advisers have often been wrong in particular situations. They have no more claim to omniscience than any other group of economic advisers; but that they have been systematically and consistently wrong is a gross exaggeration. In some cases they may have underestimated or been insensitive to the political effects of their recommendations, but, probably more often than not, they have been right.

(iii) Inadequacy of the Compensatory Financing Facility (CFF)

This IMF facility was set up in 1963 specifically to deal with a major complaint of LDCs that their export earnings were subject to severe short-term instability which disrupted their planning and damaged growth. It was considered briefly in pp 15 and 16 in Part I of this study in connection with LDCs commodity export problems.[39] The intention of the scheme was to assist LDCs in coping with balance of payments difficulties when export proceeds fell short of their expected trend level. Loans were to be repaid over the next 3 to 5 years, and preferably repayments should be made whenever export earnings rose above trend.

Initially drawings under the CFF were limited to 25 per cent of quota, were not additional to ordinary drawings, and involved the member in being prepared to co-operate with the Fund in finding

---

[38] I. Little, T. Scitovsky and M. Scott, *Industry and Trade in Some Developing Countries,* (Oxford U.P., London, 1970). A. Kreuger, *Foreign Trade Regimes and Economic Development: Liberalisation Attempts and Consequences,* (NBER, New York, 1978).

[39] Alasdair MacBean, *A Positive Approach to the International Economic Order, Part I, Trade & Structural Adjustment,* (BNAC, 1978).

"appropriate solutions for its balance of payments difficulties." Over the years the CFF has been expanded and liberalised. The last major changes were in 1975 when (1) the limit on drawings was expanded to 75 per cent of quota and could be additional to ordinary drawings; (2) the net amount by which outstanding drawings could be measured in any 12-month period was raised from 25 to 50 per cent of quota; (3) countries could draw on their ordinary quota in anticipation of the data required to establish an export shortfall and then convert this to a CFF drawing at any time up to 18 months later when data were available. The other basic features of CFF were left unchanged. Shortfalls had to be for reasons outside the country's control and the member had to co-operate with the IMF in finding solutions. The method of calculating shortfalls was based on the gap between this year's export proceeds and the average for five years encompassing the two preceding ones, the current year, and forecasts of the two subsequent years. The Fund was guided, but not bound, by this automatic formula and has in fact used its discretion in assessing shortfalls.

Probably the major criticism voiced by LDCs is that the CFF is still very inadequate in the quantity of funds it provides. They recommend a substantial increase in resources devoted to it, complete rather than partial compensation of shortfalls, inclusion of invisible earnings, calculation in real rather than nominal values, i.e. allowing for increases in the cost of imports, conversion of loans into grants after a specified period, low or zero interest terms for least developed and most seriously affected countries, and repayments from the excess of export earnings over the norm. They also contend that limitations and other restrictive conditions of access should be further relaxed.[40]

Drawings on the CFF were in fact very modest in its earlier years. Only after the conditions were significantly liberalised in 1975 did they start to rise. The major drawings have all occurred since then. They have tended to be skewed towards better-off countries. Out of the SDR 4.3 billion drawn up to 31 December 1978, 1.2 billion went to developed countries and most of the remaining 3.1 billion went to the middle income NOLDCs. Latin American countries, Malaysia, Philippines, Korea, Ivory Coast and Morocco were among the main LDC users. As long as there is little concessionality involved in these loans, which have to be repaid with interest, this distribution may not matter too much. But if poorer LDCs, despite severe (expected to be reversed) shortfalls in exports, have been unable to use the CFF because of inadequate quotas or some other barrier considered to be

---

[40] Commonwealth Experts' Group, *Towards a New International Economic Order,* (Commonwealth Secretariat, London, March 1976).

unfair, this would be a serious cause for concern. In 1976 some SDR 2.3 billion was drawn from the facility, but this met only some 10 per cent of the NOLDCs' actual aggregate export shortfall in that year. The alleged reasons for this pattern lay mainly in restricting drawings to limits based on each country's IMF quotas and partly in the exercise of discretion by Fund officials in limiting the sums lent to LDCs. It should be borne in mind that 1976 marked the middle of a world recession unprecedented in the post Second World War era, and secondly, many LDCs made extensive use of other sources of liquidity: their own reserves, stand-by arrangements and the special facilities created to deal with the oil import price emergency as well as large commercial borrowing. The fact that the CFF apparently contributed only 10 per cent to this overall shortfall does not necessarily reveal a fatal flaw in its design and operation. Data on the use made by individual countries would be more relevant.

The CFF was never intended to deal with the results of a major world recession. It is based on the assumption that the export shortfalls with which it is to deal are simply the downswings that any country can expect in the normal course of trade. Events such as the oil crisis and the subsequent world recession create too much uncertainty about future trends in export earnings to permit either individual nations or the IMF to assume that a current shortfall will be reversed in the near future. In fact commodity export earnings have not yet made any substantial recovery. Such crises need special measures and the international community has responded to some extent to provide these. The Fund in particular established several special facilities to do so, and these are considered below. The CFF as reformed in 1975 has probably done a very good job in the circumstances. The most useful change would be an increase in the size of LDCs' quotas in the Fund or a release of the CFF credits from the limitations imposed by Fund quotas. Next, calculation of shortfalls in real terms would make some allowance for the effects of inflation. But it would not be sensible to remove all Fund discretion on the amounts provided, nor, save in exceptional circumstances, to convert unpaid debts into grants. There is no logical reason for altering a facility intended to meet short term balance of payments difficulties into a means of providing long term aid. It would also be sensible, however, to make repayments obligatory when export earnings rise above trend. The trend might of course fall below previously attained peaks in real terms so repayment could be difficult and should be spread over a longer period than at present. One of the main reasons for substituting this for the present system of repayment is that a country which postpones debt repayment until a fixed date such as 3 to 5 years after receiving the credit may destabilize its net flow of foreign exchange receipts.

(iv) The Buffer Stock Financing Facility (BSFF)

The BSFF was instituted by the IMF in 1969 to assist members in financing their contributions to international buffer stocks. The LDCs' drive for a Common Fund (CF) has shown their lack of confidence in the BSFF. In fact it has been used very little and that mainly by members of the International Tin Agreement. Although set up in 1969, by the end of 1978 only SDR 66 million had been drawn for contributions to costs of financing the Tin Stocks of the ITA. Now that some form of Common Fund is likely the BSFF is probably obsolete, though it could possibly have become a viable alternative to the stock financing aspect of the CF.

(v) The Oil Facility (OF) and Subsidy Account

The OF is an *ad hoc* device set up by the IMF in 1974 to deal with the balance of payments emergency created for many of its members by the rise of oil prices and its repercussions. Access was limited in terms of quota size and willingness to consult with the Fund. It was financed by borrowing from Fund members. Interest charges have varied from 7 to $7\frac{3}{4}$ per cent. It has been a successful device for recycling some of the oil surplus money through official channels to oil importing nations. LDCs have made extensive use of it though the interest cost was an obstacle for some poor LDCs. To meet their needs the Subsidy Account was set up to reduce the interest burden for the Least Developed and Most Seriously Affected (MSA) nations.

LDCs major criticisms are that it was not enough and too expensive. Of course it did not fully compensate nations for the extra costs of oil, but it helped. NOLDCs' drawings stood at just over SDR 2.5 billion at 31 December 1978.

(vi) Extended Fund Facility (EFF) and the Trust Fund (TF)

The EFF (1975) and the TF (1976) represent two further special facilities for LDCs. The first is intended to provide medium term finance for LDCs whose balance of payments difficulties are of a nature that the economic policies required to deal with them are likely to take some time to mature. Drawings from the EFF are done in instalments which may be spread over as much as 3 years but depend on performance criteria. They can go much higher than normal stand-by arrangements, up to 140 per cent of the member's quota but as at 31 December 1978 drawings stood at only SDR 0.48 billion. Repayments can be spread over 4 to 8 years.

The Trust Fund is financed largely from gold-sales by the IMF, but supplemented by loans and voluntary contributions. It is aimed at providing concessional assistance to least developed countries in balance of payments difficulties and taking reasonable policy actions to correct their situation.

Neither of these facilities has operated for a sufficient time to provide a reliable basis for evaluation, but both go some way to meet previous LDC criticisms of lack of medium term finance and special help for the poorest LDCs.

Liquidity and/or Development: The Special Drawing Rights and their Link to Aid

For many years some academics and LDC spokesmen have argued the case for establishing a new international asset to replace, or at least supplement, gold and the key currencies as reserve assets. This case was partially accepted and the SDR was initiated with a first allocation of $10 billion over three years, of which $3.4 billion was made in the first year, 1970. But the LDCs' desire that most or all of these new assets should be issued directly to LDCs or via a development institution such as the World Bank — the Link, never gained acceptance. It has in fact been firmly opposed by the United States and West Germany.

The main role accepted for the SDR was as a method of increasing international liquidity, alternative to raising the price of gold. It was also intended to replace gradually the reserve roles of the dollar and sterling, the main reserve currencies of the 1960s and '70s. But an additional argument put by LDCs has been that, (a) LDCs had special needs for more reserves and therefore had an extra claim upon the SDRs, and (b) that they also needed extra resources to pay for capital imports from industrial countries. The difficulties of raising such revenues for transfer could be avoided by simply issuing SDRs to LDCs which they could then use to purchase the goods they needed. The SDRs would end up in the reserves of the industrial nations and the real resources would end up in the LDCs where they would assist development. But it has to be pointed out that the real resource cost to the DCs would not be avoided unless the spending of the SDRs coincided with a recession and slack capacity in the appropriate export industries in the DCs.

(i) Arguments about the Link

The debate over the aid-reserve asset link has run on over the past 20 years. LDCs succeeded in having a Joint Ministerial Committee of the IBRD and the IMF established in 1974 to consider the transfer of resources from DCs to LDCs. The preceding Committee of Twenty had indeed pronounced that "the reformed monetary system will contain arrangements to promote an increasing net flow of real resources to developing countries."[41] But the topic was subsequently dropped from the agenda of the Joint Ministerial Committee. Interest in the SDR-aid Link eroded somewhat, partly because the adoption of floating exchange rates and the expansion of the Euro-currency market have made the need for additional international liquidity seem a less pressing matter.

Two arguments, one against and the other for the SDR-aid are correct in principle, but when the probable quantities of additional SDRs are considered, both are seen to be of minor importance. The argument against an expansion of SDRs as aid is that this would be inflationary. Logically any addition to purchasing power which occurs with no matching increase in output will tend to raise prices. But SDRs are at present a very small part of international liquidity. In September 1979 SDRs amounted to only 12.5 billion as against world reserves of gold and foreign exchange (on the same date), equivalent to 296.5 billion SDRs (340.7 billion of gold were valued at market prices) or about 4 per cent. (IMF, *IFS,* December 1979). Several calculations suggest that even if 5 billion additional SDRs were issued, the resulting increment to demand for output from the OECD nations would be less than 0.3 per cent, and even if the extra demand for goods and services were concentrated on the surplus countries it would be unlikely to exceed 1.0 per cent of their total output. Such an increase is quantitatively unimportant in its effect on either inflation in a fully employed economy or in expanding demand in a world economy afflicted by recession. However, making the SDR-aid link a counter-cyclical device has on balance something to be said for it even if its effect is small. There would be a certain appeal in a device which appeared to kill three birds with one stone: add to liquidity, give aid to poor countries and help to restore employment in OECD nations in a time of recession.

Would providing aid via the Link reduce aid through other channels? This is a matter of judgement. However, if it were done simply by allocating the SDRs *directly* to all IMF members, but with more going to LDCs and even more to the poorest LDCs rather than by placing the Linked SDRs with a development agency, this aid replacement effect would be less likely. Indeed, it seems probable that extra aid would result. Furthermore, the quality of this aid might also be higher than average in some ways. It would be untied to either sources or projects. its distribution would favour the poorer LDCs by the explicit intention of the LDC proposers in the former Committee of Twenty. But it would carry interest on SDR net use. If using SDRs

---

[41] IMF, *Committee on Reform,* (Washington 1974), p 17.

involved an interest charge of 5 per cent this would mean the grant element was 33 per cent to be compared with the grant element in ODA of 80 per cent or better. There is some trade-off between the higher interest cost and the benefit of untied aid, free of political as well as economic strings.

Even were there no explicit link, LDCs would still favour additional issues of SDRs. The present international monetary system gives a 'seigniorage' advantage to the nation whose currency is used as the reserve asset, mainly the USA. It is able to gain foreign resources at relatively low cost, simply the interest it pays on dollar deposits and US stocks or bonds held by foreign countries as reserves. A gradual replacement of the dollar by the SDR would spread this gain more widely, and if poorer countries' need for additional reserves were recognised it would be better for them if they were in the form of SDRs.

Overall there seems to be a reasonable case for the Link scheme. The main worries of inflation risk and loss of control over aid seem either exaggerated or misplaced.

D. THE EXCHANGE RATE REGIME

In the early 1970s the gold exchange, fixed-rate system of exchange rates collapsed and a system of flexible rates evolved. But most LDCs have generally preferred fixed official exchange rates even when operating multiple exchange rate systems. Few of them have chosen to devalue their currencies in the face of deficits if this could possibly be avoided. Now they express a strong preference for a return to some system of fixed exchange rates backed by ample reserves in the form of SDRs.

Their preference for stable rates for their own currencies is probably sound in principle, but whether fixed rates between the industrialised nations would be in their interest is much more doubtful.

Fixed versus Floating Rates for LDCs

Paradoxically, pegged exchange rates do not necessarily mean greater trade stability. Changes in tariff rates and licensing restrictions can cause just as much uncertainty. Moreover, a pegged exchange rate is not fixed for all time and may indeed involve much larger, if less frequent, changes. In developed countries uncertainty generated by fluctuations in a free exchange rate can be reduced by the use of forward market cover. But the forward markets for many LDCs' currencies do not exist and for most they are so thin that changes in the premia or discounts over the spot rates may be too volatile to serve much purpose. This is a particular obstacle to trade among LDCs where the stability of all the currencies could be suspect and no effective forward markets may exist.

If a LDC's exchange rate fluctuates widely this may be a serious deterrent to direct investment both by foreigners and locals as there is no certainty that the capital values will rise sufficiently to compensate when its currency depreciates.

Currency fluctuations also risk stimulating destabilizing speculation. Once a government is known to be willing to permit the currency to depreciate, any adverse trade movement may lead to a massive movement out of that country's currency, precipitating an excessive fall in its value.

Finally, most LDCs do not possess powerful monetary and fiscal instruments for controlling the domestic economy. If imports, particularly food and raw materials loom large in the GDP, a currency depreciation which raises their domestic prices may trigger inflation. Nowadays, with powerful unions in some LDCs able to defend their members' real wages, it is particularly difficult to prevent a devaluation leading to domestic inflation and feeding back into a further depreciation of the exchange rate.

For all those reasons LDCs may be entirely right to prefer to fix their own exchange rates to SDRs or to their main trading partner's currency. In fact, they are free to do that — or to float — even if the rest of the world is floating. LDCs are not homogeneous, and what suits some may not suit others. But are they right to prefer that the world in general should adopt fixed rates?

Fixed Rates for the World

There are good arguments which support the LDCs' desire for stable exchange rates. First, frequent changes in industrial nations' rates can inflict losses (or gains) in the value of LDCs' portfolios of reserve assets to the extent they happen to have their reserves in the countries whose currencies happen to depreciate.

Second, if floating rates economise on the DCs' need for reserves, the demand for increased international liquidity and new issues of SDRs may be much less than in a world of pegged rates. As LDCs have an interest in more SDRs and some reasonable hopes of the SDR-aid link being achieved this slowing of SDR production would represent a blow to their legitimate interest in such increased financial resources flows to them.

But neither of these arguments is conclusive. In practice those nations whose currencies tend to depreciate usually offer high interest rates to countries which hold reserves in their depreciating currency and securities. These at least partially, if not entirely, compensate for depreciation. They may also offer good forward cover in their currencies. Further, as the bulk of LDCs' debt is denominated in the US dollar and sterling, currencies which have generally been depreciating, the reduction in the real value of their debt and its servicing costs has probably outweighed any loss on reserve values. Finally, all they need to do to avoid this risk is to diversify their reserve portfolio sensibly.

It may be true that the world may feel less need of increased official liquidity when exchange rates are more flexible and the Eurocurrency market can meet a great deal of the middle income and richer nations' requirements for short and medium term credit. But to return to the Bretton Woods ideal of rigidly pegged exchange rates in a world where countries' rates of inflation are widely varied and differences in the speed of structural change are widespread, might be to cause much greater damage to LDCs' interests.

The single most important factor in their relationships with the OECD nations is the preservation and expansion of their access to OECD markets for their exports. Both quantitatively and qualitatively this is the most crucial element in their development prospects. The preservation of a liberal trade regime is essential to that. But, fixed exchange rates force countries in payments imbalance to deflate their domestic economies and use controls on imports. Anything which increased unemployment in the OECD nations would strengthen the hands of the protectionists. As Sir Arthur Lewis the 1979 Nobel Laureate puts it:

> One has to begin by confirming the General Motors proposition (that what is good for the rich nations is also good for the poor) up to a point. LDCs require two things of More Developed Countries' currencies, and neither of these is a fixity in relationship to the other. The first requirement is that they be freely convertible into each other, so that what LDCs earn in one market they can spend in another. The second requirement is a regime within which MDCs feel comfortable, in the sense that they have no urge to restrict their imports from the rest of the world.[42]

E. CONCLUSIONS

In principle, what the developing countries need from the international monetary system is no different from the industrial nations, but for many of them the needs are more urgent. Both their exports and imports tend to be more unstable than those of richer

---

[42] Sir Arthur Lewis, "The Less Developed Countries and Stable Exchange Rates," *Third World Quarterly*, (January 1979), p 18. A fairly exhaustive account of "Exchange-rate Policy and LDCs" can be found in Chapter 12 of Graham Bird, *The International Monetary System and the Less Developed Countries*, (Macmillan 1978), a source from which some of the arguments used here are drawn.

nations and for reasons such as swings in world demand, fluctuations in harvests and changes in international prices, which are outside their control. Also, most LDCs have a large fixed element in their overseas payments: payment of interest and amortisation on past loans. This increases the burden of adjustment to a fall in exports by forcing cuts in imports needed to sustain current living standards and future growth. If the debt burden, the proportion of income and exports tied up in repayments and interest, is large, it may undermine confidence in the country's ability to service further debt, so damaging its capacity to borrow.

There was great alarm in the years after 1974 at the surge in LDC debt, occasioned by their need to pay vastly increased prices for oil imports. In the event, most of the heavy borrowing was concentrated in a few relatively successful middle income countries such as Brazil and Mexico. Rapid growth in their exports and the effects of inflation reduced the real burden of servicing their debts and kept it manageable. Very few countries got into serious trouble up to 1978. But the further sharp rise in oil prices in 1978/79 has increased the risk of defaults and a consequent general crisis in banking confidence once more. It is in the DCs' interest, just as much as in the LDCs, to avoid such a crisis. It would severely worsen the recession into which the world is already moving.

As there are some doubts as to the willingness or ability of the commercial banks to meet the needs to channel oil surplus and OECD funds to LDCs in the way they have done in 1974-76, there is a need to ease LDCs' access to official funds. For some LDCs 'bunching' of repayments could cause a crisis. These need to be identified and some of their loans converted into longer term loans with interest adjustments to ensure equal treatment of debtors and creditors. Special institutional arrangements probably under the IMF would be needed for this. Various reforms to ease access to IMF funds are possible and should be initated.

For most of the poorer LDCs, commercial loans are neither the problem nor the solution. Their debts are mainly the result of official development assistance. They have received some help through recent conversions of past loans into grants by the majority of OECD nations. For most of them the problem is not one of access to short term finance but of inadequate long term finance for development. Debt remission is one way of providing them with untied funds, but much more new grant or very soft loan aid is required to finance technical assistance and capital to assist progress in their economies. To meet increased costs of oil they need to be able to borrow on easy terms from official sources.

As far as international monetary arrangements are concerned an exchange regime which facilitates the trade and restored growth of the industrial nations is also crucial to the LDCs as their prosperity is still largely dependent on their trade with DCs.

Improved access to IMF resources, especially further reforms of the Compensatory Financing Facility and expansion of the resources of the new Supplementary Financing (Witteveen) facility, together with the introduction of the 'Link' are changes which could bring important benefits to all LDCs and would help to sustain world demand during periods of recession.

Appendix to Chapter II

COMPARISON OF INSTABILITY FOR LDCs' EXPORTS AND IMPORTS

The IMF and Coppock results were confirmed by fresh calculations for various periods: 1950-59, 1960-69, 1970-75 and for the whole period 1960-75.

Indices of Instability

	1950-59	1960-69	1970-75	1960-75
Exports	13.2	12.2	16.2	32.9
Imports	43.8	21.0	12.9	47.6

In each case save 1970-75 the mean instability index for exports was smaller than for imports for a sample which included all the LDCs for which data were available (126).

The index of instability used was
$$\frac{1}{n}\sum\left(\frac{x-\bar{x}}{\bar{x}}\right)^2 \times 100$$

where x = recorded value of exports or imports

$\bar{x}$ = trend value of exports estimated by an exponential trend fitted by least squares method.

For further details contact A. I. MacBean, University of Lancaster.

I am grateful to Tin and Huan Nguyen for the data analysis and calculations involved in this.

III. Foreign Direct Investment and International Transfer of Technology

A. INTRODUCTION

The role of private foreign direct investment (FDI) in the development process has been the subject of considerable discussion. It has figured prominently in the North-South dialogue and was high on the agenda of several recent UN conferences including the 1979 conference on Science, Technology and Development.

Foreign direct investment is an area rich in controversy. Its supporters believe that it can not only contribute capital to the recipients but also impart additional benefits in the form of technology and managerial skills. Indeed, a distinguishing characteristic of FDI, especially since the rise of the multinational enterprise (MNE), is the technology and managerial skills that accompany it. It is thus that technology transfers form an integral part of most discussions on FDI. That the multinational enterprise is an effective conduit of technology to the developing countries is generally accepted. But the relative costs and benefits of its operations to the developing countries form a matter of intense debate.

To its opponents the multinational enterprise is an instrument of exploitation, the epitome of the evils of capitalism. Its sheer size, its geographical spread and ease of access to resources are seen to pose a threat to the economic and political sovereignty of the newly independent nations of the Third World. To its protagonists, the MNE is the major agent of change, a vehicle *par excellence* for the dissemination of the fruits of science and technology, and one of the main instruments for an integrated world order. And the MNEs for their part see themselves as neutral agents of capital and technology transfer, possessing little or no power over the destinies of the countries in which they invest.

The developing countries caught between these opposing views have adopted an ambivalent attitude towards foreign direct investment. This is clearly reflected in the 1974 declaration on the New International Economic Order (NIEO)[43] which is generally hostile to foreign direct investment. The hostility is tempered by the recognition that foreign direct investment, especially in its technological contribution, has a role in the development process. The main thrust of the declaration is towards reform and regulation and not a radical rejection of foreign owned enterprise participation in developing countries.

The issues posed in the declaration for FDI cover a wide

---

[43] UN Press Release, May 1974, "Declaration on the New International Economic Order".

spectrum. They range from the pricing of imported technologies to the need for an international code of conduct on transfers of them. The oft repeated criticisms that too little of the rewards of foreign direct investment accrue to the host countries, that the technology transmitted by the foreign firms are inappropriate to the developing countries and that foreign firms engage in unfair commercial practices are all implicit in the demands made in the declaration. While there may be more than a modicum of truth in these grievances much of it also arises out of emotive considerations and an insufficient understanding of the economic forces underlying foreign private investment and technology transmission. While there may be undesirable practices that some of the multinationals are answerable for, there is also the danger that hasty and ill-conceived regulations and restrictions may undermine their acknowledged ability to effect capital and technology transfers. The central issue is how best to harness the prowess of the multinational enterprise as an agent of change without, in the process, undermining its very capability to do so.

There is a considerable and highly controversial literature on the role of FDI in the developing countries. But very little of it is factual and objective. This chapter evaluates the contribution of FDI to the development process, identifies the mutual benefits from FDI to the foreign firms and the developing countries and analyses the claims of developing countries in the light of available facts and empirical evidence. The discussion in this chapter is confined to FDI in the manufacturing sector.[44]

B. SIZE AND PATTERN OF FOREIGN DIRECT INVESTMENT IN THE DEVELOPING COUNTRIES

Size

An important feature of foreign direct investment is that much of it is undertaken by a limited number of multinational enterprises. A working definition of an MNE is one which owns or controls producing facilities in more than one country. Around 171 enterprises accounted in 1971 for more than 50 per cent of all foreign direct investment and these are based in five main investing countries. (Appendix Table 1).

Data on production and exports also shows a similar pattern of concentration in large size MNEs. The value added of all multinationals estimated at $500 billion in 1971, was about one fifth of

---

[44] For a discussion of the issues peculiar to foreign direct investment in the extractive sectors of LDCs see R. F. Mikesell, *New Patterns of World Mineral Development*, (BNAC, 1979).

world gross national product, excluding that of the centrally planned economies. The US tariff commission estimates show that in 1970 US multinationals alone accounted for 25 per cent of world exports of all commodities and about 20 per cent of world exports of manufactures.

Several other data, such as the concentration of R and D expenditures in the hands of multinationals, could be cited to attest to their economic strength and flexibility of operations. It is, however, sufficient to note that it is this concentration of economic power which is seen to pose a threat to the economic independence and political sovereignty of the developing countries. Beyond that is the apparent perceived inability of LDCs to bargain effectively with the multinationals over the sharing of the awards from foreign direct investment.

In absolute terms the world stock of foreign direct investment in the developing countries is not very high. The total at the end of the year 1975 was estimated at around $259 billion with the developing countries' share at $68 billion (26 per cent of the total).[45] However, compared to the total level of output, foreign direct investment is much more important to the developing countries as a group than for developed countries. The ratio of the stock of foreign direct investment to GNP at the end of the year 1970 was 0.090 for all developing countries and 0.059 for developed countries.[46]

Recent estimates published by the OECD show a rising trend in the flow of foreign direct investment to the developing countries. Between the years 1970 and 1976 the annual average rate of growth of such investment was around 13 per cent and at the end of the year 1976 the total stock of FDI in the developing countries had increased to $76 billion.[47] It is also to be noted that in 1976 foreign direct investments formed nearly 40 per cent of all private capital flows.

The Major Investors

The only comprehensive source of data on the share of different countries in the total stock of foreign direct investment in the developing countries is that published by the UN for the year 1967 and some of this data has been updated by UN Commission on Transnational Corporation in 1978. In 1967 (the year for which comprehensive data for source country and host regions are available) the US accounted for 50 per cent of the total investment with the bulk of it concentrated in Latin America, followed by the UK with a 20 per

---

[45] *Transnational Corporations in World Development; A Re-examination,* (UN, New York, 1978).

[46] Grant L. Reuber et al *Private Foreign Investment in Development,* (Oxford, Clarendon Press, 1973) p 94.

[47] *Development Co-operation* DAC, *1978 Review, op. cit.,* (OECD, Paris, 1978).

cent share, much of it concentrated in Asia and Africa. The remaining 30 per cent is accounted for principally by Japan, West Germany and France. (Table 3:1).

However, in recent years, Japan and West Germany have been rapidly increasing their share. An examination of the ratio of the annual increase of foreign investment flows to GDP of various investing countries, suggests that West Germany and Japan are internationalising their production facilities at the same rate as the US. It is also of significance that US investors are increasingly directing their investments to Asia and Africa. During the period 1961 to 1971 'only' 56 per cent of new US affiliates in manufacturing in the developing countries were located in Latin America, their traditional stronghold; the remainder were located in Africa, Asia and Oceania.[48] These trends point to growing competition among the investing countries for the markets in developing countries. This may reduce the degree of dependence of the developing countries on any one source for their needs of technology and capital.

The Recipients

Among the developing regions Latin America is the major recipient of FDI. However, in recent years there has been a marked increase in the share of the Asian countries. (Table 3:2).

A feature of FDI in the developing countries is its concentration in a few countries in each of the major regions. At the end of the year 1967 Brazil, Venezuela, Argentina and Mexico together accounted for nearly 59 per cent of the total stock of FDI in Latin America. In Asia, India, the Philippines, Malaysia, Pakistan and Hong Kong accounted for 67 per cent of the total stock of investment in the region. Similarly in Africa, Nigeria, Algeria, Libya, Zaire and Zambia accounted for 50 per cent of the total stock of FDI in the region. The estimates for 1976 show that the pattern has not altered much, though Brazil and Mexico in the Latin American region and Indonesia, Hong Kong, Singapore and Korea in the Asian region have experienced an appreciable increase in the inflow of FDI. (Table 3.3)

---

[48] Bernard Mennis and Karl P. Sauvant, *Emerging Forms of Transnational Community,* (London, Lexington Books, 1976) p 11.

Table 3.1

**Stock of Foreign Direct Investment in Developing Countries
by Region and Country of Origin, 1967**

Recipient Region Country of Origin	Middle East	Asia	Africa	Latin America	Total
A. Distribution of Total Stock by Region ($ billions) (percent of total)	$3.1 9.4%	$5.0 15.0%	$6.6 20.0%	$18.4 55.6%	$33.1 100.0%
B. Distribution of Regional Totals by Country of Origin All Countries	100.0%	100.0%	100.0%	100.0%	100.0%
U.S.A	57.3	35.6	20.8	63.8	50.4
U.K.	27.1	41.5	30.0	9.2	19.9
France	5.2	6.6	26.3	2.5	8.1
Netherlands	5.6	5.1	4.9	5.1	5.1
Canada	0.2	1.0	0.7	7.3	3.1
Japan	2.7	3.9	0.2	2.2	2.1
Italy	0.8	0.6	3.8	2.1	2.7
Belgium	0.1	0.3	7.3	0.6	1.9
Switzerland	0.2	1.4	0.9	2.3	1.7
Others	0.1	2.6	3.0	0.6	1.3

Source: *Multinational Corporations in World Development* (New York: United Nations, 1973)

Table 3.2

**Regional Distribution of Stock of Foreign
Direct Investment in Developing Countries**

	1967		1976	
	Total stock	Share of Recipient Regions	Total stock	Share of Recipient Regions
	(Billion $)	(per cent)	(Billion $)	(per cent)
All Developing Countries	33.1	100	76.2	100
Latin America	18.4	56	33.3	43
Asia	5.0	15	19.2	25
Middle East	3.1	9	2.6	3

Source: 1967 figures from U.N. *Multinational Corporations in World Development* (New York 1973).
1976 figures estimated from data in *Development Co-operation, DAC 1978 Review,* (OECD, Paris, 1978).

This geographic concentration of foreign direct investment is to be explained by the sectoral composition of such investment, the economic policies of host countries and the 'climate' they provide for such investment. FDI is concentrated in the petroleum and manufacturing sectors. At the end of 1972, the latest year for which detailed data are available on all investors, 35 per cent of the total stock of foreign direct investment in the developing countries was in petroleum, 30 per cent in manufacturing and 10 per cent in mining. (Appendix Table 2).

The petroleum and mineral resource endowments of the main recipients in Africa accounts for the concentration of foreign direct investment in these countries. Much of the investment in the Latin American and Asian countries, with the exception of Venezuela, is in manufacturing. Brazil, Argentina, Mexico, India and Spain, the so-called 'Big Five' developing countries, account for nearly 60 per cent of all foreign investment in manufacturing in the developing countries. These countries have had a long history of industrialisation and the accent of their industrialisation programmes is on technologically intensive sectors such as steel, chemicals, pharmaceuticals and transport equipment. The import substituting industrialisation policies pursued by these countries have also provided the foreign firms with profitable markets sheltered from international competition

Table 3.3

**Distribution among LDCs of the Stock
of Foreign Direct Investment** (per cent)

	1967	1976
Latin America	**100%**	**100%**
Brazil	20.2	27.3
Venezuela	18.9	8.7
Argentina	9.9	6.8
Mexico	9.7	14.0
Others	41.3	43.2
Asia	**100%**	**100%**
India	26.2	13.0
Philippines	14.5	7.3
Malaysia	13.6	12.5
Pakistan	6.9	4.0
Hong Kong	5.7	7.7
Indonesia	5.1	26.6
Thailand	4.3	1.8
Singapore	3.7	6.9
South Korea	1.6	6.0
Others	18.4	14.2
Africa	**100%**	**100%**
Nigeria	16.8	10.4
Algeria	10.7	4.1
Libya	8.8	5.1
Zaire	7.3	11.5
Zambia	6.4	3.1
Kenya	2.6	5.2
Others	47.4	67.6

Source: UN *Multinational Corporations in World Development* (New York, 1973) for 1967 figures.
For 1976, estimated on the basis of data in *Development Co-operation,* DAC *1978 Review,*
(OECD, Paris, 1978).

by tariffs and quotas. This is a point of significance in the analysis of
benefit sharing and capital-intensity of foreign firms discussed in the
ensuing sections. It is also to be noted that the sectoral composition of
foreign direct investment in LDCs is changing increasingly in favour of
manufacturing and services and away from petroleum and mining.
Recent data for US investment shows this trend to be vivid since 1970.
(Appendix Table 3).

A salient feature of foreign direct investment in the manufacturing sector, whose ramifications have been the focus of debate, is its orientation towards exports. Although such export oriented investment is mainly in Korea, Taiwan, Hong Kong and Singapore, it is also gathering strength in Mexico, Brazil and India. The relatively liberal policies towards foreign private investment pursued by these countries, and their extensive use of 'international sub-contracting' arrangements explains the massive surge of investment into these countries. (Appendix Table 4). This aspect is discussed in detail later.

The foregoing statistics, though scant in many respects, highlight the important features of foreign direct investment in the developing countries. First, foreign direct investment continues to be concentrated in a few developing countries. For instance in 1975 ten developing countries accounted for 40.6 per cent of the total stock of FDI in the developing countries compared with 36.5 per cent in 1976 and 37 per cent in 1971.[49] Second, despite all the clamour for regulations on foreign direct investment by the developing countries, there is a rising trend in the flow of FDI to these countries. Third, foreign direct investment is shifting towards the technologically intensive manufacturing industries and the services sector and away from their traditional strongholds of plantations, mining and petroleum.

The lack of detailed and up-to-date statistical data on the size and pattern of FDI in developing countries is regrettable.

C. SHARING THE REWARDS

The heart of the debate on foreign direct investment is the sharing of its rewards between the foreign firms and the host countries. Indeed, most criticisms of FDI in terms of the inappropriateness of its technologies, its packaged nature, monopolistic pricing of products and technologies are merely symptomatic of the concern in the developing countries that the foreign firms garner a disproportionate share of the rewards.

The presumption that the incursion of a package of capital, technology and managerial skills must increase the economic welfare of the host countries is questioned by critics of MNEs on several grounds. Foreign direct investment, it is argued, may merely replace domestic investment. In its absence domestic investment could have generated an equivalent amount of employment and income. The technology and skills FDI imparts, far from being an asset, may be a liability. The capital-intensive nature of such technology may limit

---

[49] *Transnational Corporations in World Development – a Re-examination:* (UN, 1978), Table III. p 47.

Table 3.4

**Retained Value Added on Account of US Foreign
Direct Investment in Developing Regions**

| | Latin America | | | | Far East (excl. Japan) | |
| | 1957 | | 1966 | | 1957 | |
	$ Million	%	$ Million	%	$ Million	%
Wages & Salaries	380	19	810	18	33	15
Tax revenues (including Miscellaneous Payments)	301	15	761	17	24	11
Expenditures on local materials and equipment	1,330	66	2,955	65	162	74
Total retained value added	2,011	100	4,526	100	219	100

Source: G. L. Reuber et al *Private Foreign Investment in Development* for the OECD (Oxford University Press 1973) p 150.

labour absorption. Furthermore, it is alleged that the returns earned by foreign firms bear no relation to the costs they incur in producing such technologies. The problem is compounded if the MNEs indulge in pricing practices which evade local taxes on their profits.

Much ink has been spilled on theories and conjectures of this sort. But little effort has been expended in quantifying the actual share of the rewards accruing to the developing countries from existing FDI. There is little reliable data for such an exercise. But what there is, is worth examining before analysing the issues raised above.

The Rewards of the Developing Countries

(i) Tangible Gains

The major tangible gains that accrue to the developing countries from foreign direct investment are (a) the tax revenues it generates, (b) the expenditures foreign firms incur in buying local materials and components, and (c) the payments they make for local labour services.[50] Together, these three items amount to the value added retained by the host country or 'retained value added'.

One of the few pieces of evidence on retained value added is provided by an OECD study by Grant Reuber in 1973. This reports that retained value added on account of US direct investment in Latin America was 82.9 per cent of the total value of sales in 1957 and had increased to around 90 per cent by 1966. For the Far East this figure was around 88 per cent in 1957 (Table 3.4).

Expenditures on local materials and equipment constitute the biggest component of retained value added. Such expenditures tend to be high in the case of home market oriented investments compared to export oriented investments. But much of the home market oriented investments may be of the import-substitution variety undertaken in response to tariffs and quotas on imports imposed by the host countries. In many of these cases it is possible that the developing countries would have been better off importing the products than allowing foreign firms to produce them behind tariff walls. The resources tied up in the import-substituting industries could be used in other activities where the developing countries may have a comparative advantage. Import substituting investment may result in resource misallocation irrespective of whether the investment is undertaken by locally-owned firms or foreign firms. But in the case of the latter the tax revenues they generate may provide some off-set to the resource misallocation costs. The developing countries could gain

---

[50] It may be argued that it is the number of jobs foreign firms create rather than the wage bill that is more relevant to developing countries. The employment aspect is discussed in the next section.

something from the taxes they can impose on the capital and auxilliary services provided by the foreign firms.

Indeed, tax revenues constitute one of the important tangible gains from FDI to the developing countries. These accounted for around 17 per cent of the total retained value added for US investment in Latin America in 1966 and 13 per cent for the Far East (Table 4). Detailed and up-to-date statistics on this aspect are again not available. One estimate for the year 1970 puts the total tax revenues accruing to the developing countries on account of FDI at $5.5 billion to £7.0 billion.[51] Manufacturing investment accounts for around 30 per cent of this total. This sum which constitutes around 3 to 4 per cent of the national income of the developing countries is considerable.

The wage and salary payments made by the foreign firms is the other major tangible reward from FDI to the developing countries. This accounts for around 15 to 18 per cent of retained value added. In general an increase in capital stock enhances labour income through increased employment and increased wages and salaries. There is some evidence in support of the argument that foreign owned enterprises tend to pay relatively high wage rates. In a sample of twenty-three FDI projects in developing countries it was found that fifteen paid 1 to 10 per cent above going wage rates and eight paid more than 10 per cent above going wage rates.[52] Such a wage policy by the foreign firms may reflect their need for skilled labour and a desire to appease local trade union sentiments against their operations. But it could also reflect payments made for scarce labour skills.

(ii) Other rewards

A second set of rewards from FDI to the host countries, ones less tangible and therefore difficult to measure, are spin-offs of technology, labour and managerial skills. Although such 'external economies' cannot be quantified, they are nevertheless discernible. For instance, if labour and management trained by foreign firms subsequently leave for other local enterprises there would be a clear social gain to the host countries as the skills would have been obtained at no cost to the country. Foreign firms are often a fertile training ground for prospective local enterpreneurs.

Sub-contracting arrangements between foreign-owned enterprises and local producers of components and equipment is another channel for the diffusion of technology. More often then not

---

[51] *The Impact of Multinational Enterprises on Employment and Training,* (ILO, Geneva, 1976) p 19.
[52] Reuber et al, *Foreign Private Investment in Development,* (Oxford University Press, 1973) p 175.

foreign firms entering into such arrangements provide the local firms with technical assistance, blueprints, designs and drawings. In cases where the host governments stipulate that the foreign firms should purchase a proportion of their inputs locally, it would be in the interests of the foreign firms to ensure that the quality of inputs they purchase meet their required standards.

The foregoing shows that considerable benefits accrue to the host countries from the operations of foreign firms. But could they have been greater? Have the foreign firms managed to skim a disproportionate share of the rewards by monopolistic pricing policies and various other ruses to avoid local taxes? Before examining these questions the share of the rewards accruing to the foreign investors must be examined.

The Rewards to the Investor

(i) Rates of Return on Capital

The major reward from FDI to the investors is the return on capital they are able to earn. The conceptual problems associated with the valuation of capital are well known, and book values of capital estimated at their historic cost of acquisition may rarely reflect their replacement value. Furthermore, when a particular foreign subsidiary is but one cog in the world-wide operations of the MNE it is difficult to evaluate returns on each investment. The reported rates of return on capital of foreign firms may, therefore, be under- or over-, stated.

These qualifications have to be borne in mind when assessing the rates of return on FDI. Table 3.5 sets out the comparative rates of return on the stock of US foreign direct investment in the manufacturing sectors of developed and developing countries. Figures produced in the Reddaway Report for UK manufacturing investment abroad[53] show the average annual rate of return on capital for the years 1965-68 to be 9.8 per cent in the developed countries and. These estimates do not show an appreciable difference between the rates of return earned by foreign firms in either type of host country.

(ii) Royalties and technical fees

Royalties and technical fees paid by firms in the developing countries are another form of reward for the investor. A distinction must be made between the royalty and fee payments made by the subsidiaries to their parent firms and such payments made by unaffiliated domestic firms to foreign firms for imports of technology. In the former case the royalty and fee payments made by the

---

[53] W. B. Reddaway et al, *UK Direct Investment Overseas; Final Report,* (Cambridge 1968).

Table 3.5

Rates of Return on US Foreign Private Investment
in Manufacturing (per cent)

	1970	**1975**	**1976**	**1977**	**1978**
Developing countries	10.5	10.6	12.5	11.7	15.6
Developing countries	10.8	13.9	11.5	11.1	14.7

Note: Rate of return is defined as income (sum of dividends, interest payments, earnings of unincorporated affiliates) plus reinvested earnings of incorporated affiliates divided by the average of the beginning and the end of the year stock of foreign private investment.

Source: US Department of Commerce, *Survey of Current Business,* various issues.

subsidiaries may be profits disguised as costs. If such payments attract a lower tax rate it pays the foreign firm to transfer abroad some of its profits in the form of royalty and fee payments.

Admittedly royalties and fee payments offer an attractive route to the foreign firms to transfer income out of the host countries. Especially so if such payments are subject to little or no taxes or if the dividend repatriation route is constrained by host government legislation. It is reported that nearly 34 per cent of the income received by US firms from their operations abroad was in the form of royalties and technical fees.[54]

However, it may be an exaggeration to say that all of the royalties and fee payments constitute disguised profits. A substantial part of such payments may represent inter affiliate charges for technology supplied by the parent to the subsidiary, which is one method by which the subsidiary could be made to bear its share of the managerial and technology costs. Often in the initial years of operation the subsidiaries are charged very little or nothing at all for the managerial and technical services they obtain from the parent; growing subsidiaries are required to pay their way through. This suggests that royalties and fee payments are not always a method of repatriating profits.

However, if all such payments are regarded as profits and added to the income of the foreign firms their rate of return on capital goes up from the reported 11 per cent to 14 per cent of book value. This could not be judged excessive considering the comparable rate of return on capital earned at home by the foreign firms is also around 14 per cent.

These then are the rewards from FDI which flow to the developing countries and foreign firms alike. This, however, is not the whole story.

---

[54] Sidney M. Robbins and Robert B. Stobaugh, *Money in the Multinational Enterprise: A Study of Financial Policy,* (Longman, 1974).

The developing countries have expressed considerable dissatisfaction at the share of rewards accruing to the foreign firms.

The Dispute over Rewards

A series of allegations have been made by developing countries which are difficult to prove but which bedevil all discussion of the topic. Put briefly these are: (i) imported technologies are excessively priced; (ii) the developing countries are deprived of their share of tax revenues because of transfer pricing practices on the part of foreign firms.

(i) Technology Pricing

The argument that foreign firms 'exploit' developing countries is long standing, taking all sorts of shapes and forms. Exploitation is an emotionally charged concept. Strictly interpreted economic exploitation arises when the returns to the firms are much higher than that which they could earn elsewhere on comparable projects or when they far exceed their contribution to the economy. Demonstration of such exploitation requires relating of costs to benefits. On the costs side data estimated by the UNCTAD show that in the year 1968 payments for imports of technology by developing countries amounted to 0.47 per cent of their GDP, 5 per cent of their non-petroleum export earnings, 25 per cent of official aid flows and 56 per cent of inflows of capital on account of foreign direct investment.[55] On the basis of this data it is suggested that payments for imported technology have been excessive and impose a balance of payments burden on the developing countries. But no attempt is made by the UNCTAD to relate these costs to the stream of tangible and intangible benefits conferred by imported technologies in the form of increased productivity, labour and managerial skills.[56]

Several of the developing countries, however, have in recent years started to regulate foreign royalty payments, made by both subsidiaries and unaffiliated firms. Such a policy is motivated by the belief that imported technologies are excessively priced. But when there are no comparable arm's-length prices applicable to such transactions there is no standard by which to judge whether or not the prices charged for imported technologies are excessive.

Only conjectural answers are possible to this conundrum. One criticism is that the returns earned by foreign firms on the sale of their

---

[56] *Major Issues Arising from the Transfer of Technology to Developing Countries,* (UNCTAD, Geneva, 1975).

[56] For a detailed discussion of the UNCTAD arguments see V.N. Balasubramanyam "International Transfer of Technology: UNCTAD Arguments in Perspective", *World Economy.* (Oct. 1977) Vol. I.

technology are inordinately excessive in view of the fact that the marginal cost of producing knowledge is zero. This thesis is an example of misapplication of economic theory to the analysis of foreign private investment. In theory the marginal cost of replicating an existing invention is trivial compared to the average costs of research and development. If the invention were sold on the open market it would become freely available as it can be reproduced at little or no cost. Because the marginal cost of reproducing existing inventions may be trivial, it is argued that in order to maximise the social benefits arising from the production of knowledge it should be freely transmitted without limit instead of monopolising it and charging for it. Hence the argument that the multinationals are garnering unearned rents by monopolising and charging for knowledge which ought to be a free good.

There is, however, a world of difference between what ought to be and what can be. It could be argued that ideally the state should invest in the production of knowledge and distribute it free of charge to the users. But this may be a far cry. It must be noted that State funded R and D is not costless. It has to be financed from government revenues and resources may have to be transferred from other areas to finance it. In any case much of the basic research is funded by the State and conducted in Universities and non-profit research institutions. The results are 'freely' available in journals, and research reports lodged in libraries and elsewhere. But the application of such knowledge to industrial and commercial uses is developed by manufacturing firms at a cost and therefore their preserve. By its very nature 'applied' research cannot be divested from the business of manufacturing and marketing. Such being the case, private profit maximising firms can hardly be expected to function as public service agencies devoted to the free dissemination of knowledge. Deprived of returns to their research and development activity, they would have no incentive to engage in the continued production of knowledge. If society is to benefit from the continued production of knowledge, incentives to such production have to be preserved. When firms find that they are unable to reap the full benefits flowing from their R and D activities, they may proceed to internalise operations by setting up production facilities abroad. In other words firms expand to internalise the externalities inherent in the production and sale of knowledge.

A sizeable proportion of the profits made by the foreign firms may, therefore, represent returns to their past investment in research and development. It is also to be recognised that R and D has to bear the risks of failure and manufacturing firms have to be rewarded for bearing such risks. Further, there are also costs to transferring technology from one production locale to another. These costs could be considerable in the case of complex technologies which require the transfer of human skills to make the knowledge embodied in tangibles like blueprints, designs and equipment operative. In a case study of 26 transfer projects relating to chemicals, petroleum refining and machinery industries, transfer costs were found to be in the range of 2 to 59 per cent of the total costs of the projects, with the average for all projects around 19 per cent.[57] This variation between projects is accounted for by differences in the nature of technology transferred, the age of the technology and the absorptive capacity of the technology recipient firms.

The foregoing has argued that what is often regarded as monopoly profits may constitute no more than a reward to past investments in research and development. Also it is a necessary price to pay for the continued production of knowledge. Even so, there may be an element of truth in the argument that the developing countries have been forced to bear a disproportionate share of this burden. In the absence of information on what they are buying they may have struck a poor bargain.

In such cases what is needed is more information to purchasers on alternative sources and streams of technologies. Developing countries are in this regard better placed now than they were in the 1950s. Their bargaining strength has grown, both because of learning by doing and increased competition among suppliers of technology. Entry by Japan and the West European countries into the market as sellers of technology has considerably whittled down the monopoly held by US firms in many of the technologically intensive industries. For example, in the chemical engineering industy, although business has expanded ten fold over the past 20 years, the US share of the business has dropped from nearly 100 per cent to less than 50 per cent.[58]

Another important source of 'monopoly profit' to the foreign firms arises from the import substituting industrialisation policies of many of the developing countries. Any element of 'monopoly' in the profits of the foreign firms may reflect the high protection from international competition afforded by these policies. In the case of some countries like India, domestic industrial licensing policies have accentuated the problem by also limiting competition from domestically owned firms. Clearly in these cases the onus of the blame for any monopoly profits enjoyed by foreign firms rests on the developing countries themselves. The obvious remedy in these cases is

---

[57] See D. J. Teece, "Technology Transfer my Multinational Firms: The Resource Cost of Transferring Technological Know-how", *Economic Journal*, (June 1977).

[58] J. Baranson, *Technology and the Multinationals* (D. C. Heath and Company, Lexington, Mass. 1978) Ch. 6, p147.

to promote competition by following outward looking policies and lowering the degree of protection afforded to the foreign firms.

(ii) The Practice of Transfer Pricing

It is generally accepted that it is possible for foreign firms to shift profits from one area of operation to another by disguising them as costs of equipment and materials sold to their subsidiaries. If this was being done, the prices charged for such equipment could differ substantially from those that obtain under 'arm's-length' transactions. The prices can therefore be manipulated to transfer profits from one area of operations to another depriving host or home governments of tax revenues.

Several questions arise on this issue. Firstly, how extensive are such practices? Secondly, what precisely is the motivation for them? And, finally, what can be done to mitigate them?

The basic objective of a multinational enterprise is to minimise costs throughout the organisation, to which end it is likely to employ all the tools in the financial kit. Transfer pricing provides one such means and some multinationals have been shown to engage in using it to that end.[59] The main motivation for such use of transfer pricing arises from international differences in tax and tariff rates, host government restrictions on profit repatriation and regulations on royalty rates and technical fees. Risk minimisation may also play a role. Threats of nationalisation, anticipated balance of payments problems, and the need to keep a low profit profile in the host countries may also motivate the foreign firms to engage in using transfer pricing to hide profits.

The most commonly recognised determinants of such uses of transfer pricing are international differences in tax and tariff rates. If the host country's tariff rates are low and profit tax rates high relative to the home country of the enterprise, it may find it advantageous to over-price its exports to the subsidiaries.

But paradoxically it is the governments of the developed countries, principally the US, that appear to be as concerned about the misuse of transfer pricing as LDCs. Their complaint is that the incidence of taxes on the subsidiaries of multinationals in the developing countries tend to be low, resulting in an underpricing of exports to the subsidiaries. This enables the multinationals to declare a high proportion of their profits in the host countries. Various developments in the United States, such as the setting up by the Inland Revenue Service of the Office of International Operations, are in response to this complaint by the US government. Further, an

---

[59] Sidney M. Robbins and Robert B. Stobaugh, *op. cit.*

extensive survey of the available literature on the practice of transfer pricing also suggests that in practice tax rate differentials are not the main factor motivating unfair transfer pricing practices.[60]

The principal encouragement for this practice appears to be non-fiscal incentives, especially ceilings imposed by the host countries on repatriation of profits, royalty rates and technical fees. That such is the case is also suggested by the two widely quoted pieces of empirical evidence on transfer pricing relating to Colombia. Sanjaya Lall's estimates show that overpricing of imported inputs in the foreign owned pharmacuetical firms in Colombia ranged from 33 per cent to more that 300 per cent of international market prices, during the years 1966-70.[61] Similarly, Constantine Vaitsos has reported overpricing of pharmaceutical products averaging 155 per cent, rubber products averaging 40 per cent, chemicals 25.5 per cent and electronics in the range of 16 to 60 per cent.[62] These estimates also relate to Colombia for the year 1968.

The accuracy of these estimates has been criticised for the underlying weakness of the data on which they are based. But that the practice prevails can hardly be questioned. However, such practices in Colombia appear to have been heavily influenced by the Colombian government's ceilings on repatriation of dividends. It should also be noted that the evidence relates mainly to the pharmaceutical industry and both developed and developing countries have been concerned about transfer pricing practices of MNEs in this industry.

If the motivation for the practice identified above is correct, it suggests that the developing countries may not be able to gain much by imposing ceilings on dividend repatriation. It also suggests a need for co-ordination of policies among different tax authorities in the host countries. These and other possible remedies for the problem of transfer pricing are discussed in a later section of this chapter.

To sum up, there is clearly mutual benefit in practice from foreign direct investment. The criticism by the developing countries that they tend to be monopolistically exploited by the foreign firms appears to be an exaggeration. This criticism arises from misconceptions regarding the nature of the multinational enterprise and misapplication of economic theory to analysis of the pricing of technologies. The element of 'monopoly' that does exist in the profits made by the foreign firms is

---

[60] George F. Kopitz: "Taxation and Multinational Firm Behaviour", *IMF Staff Papers*, Vol. XXIII, No. 3, (Nov. 1976).

[61] Sanjaya Lall, "Transfer Pricing by Multinational Manufacturing Firms", *Oxford Bulletin of Economics and Statistics,* Vol. 35, (August 1973).

[62] C. Vaitsos, *Inter-Country Income Distribution and Transnational Enterprises,* (Oxford, Clarendon Press, 1974).

mainly a result of lack of information on the part of the developing countries and their protectionist policies.

D.   EMPLOYMENT ASPECTS

What has been

Much of the controversy surrounding foreign direct investment is in the realm of speculation; on what could have been rather than what has been or is. This is particularly so in the case of employment effects of foreign investment. The issue is crystallized in the question: Could job creation have been higher in the absence of such investment?

The UN Commission for Transnational Corporations has estimated that the total number of persons directly employed by foreign affiliates in the developing countries was between 3 and 4 million in 1976.[63] This constitutes a bare 1.0 per cent of the labour force in the developing countries. But as a proportion of the total number 100 million unemployed in these countries, it is nearly 4 per cent. In fact this figure may be an underestimate as it excludes the indirect employment effects of such investment, which could be substantial, depending on the extent of the linkages between the foreign firms and the host economies. As already noted above the bulk of FDI is concentrated in a relatively few developing countries. The pertinent point in discussions of the employment effects of FDI therefore is the consequent job creation in these countries. Unfortunately, such data are not generally available in sufficient detail to come to incontrovertible conclusions. However, the available figures for Mexico and Brazil show that the multinationals there have made significant contribution to employment. The share of foreign direct investment in the total manufacturing investment in these countries is around 30 per cent.[64] In Brazil the share of multinational enterprises in total manufacturing employment increased from 6.7 per cent in 1966 to 8.5 per cent in 1970. For Mexico the comparable figures are 6.5 per cent and 9.9 per cent. Further, the rate of growth of employment in the multinationals in these countries was much higher than that in the nationally owned enterprises. In Mexico over the period 1965-70 for the manufacturing sector as a whole employment in multinationals increased at 12 per cent per annum compared to 1.5 per cent in the case of nationally owned enterprises.[65]

Further evidence on the job creation potential of FDI comes from the experience of South Asian countries like South Korea, Singapore

---

[63] Transnational Corporations in World Development: a Re-examination (UN, New York, 1978).

[64] *Impact of Multinational Enterprises on Employment and Training* (ILO, Geneva, 1976), pp 8-9.

[65] *Ibid.*, p9

and Hong Kong. As already noted, FDI in these countries is heavily oriented towards exports and much of it is of the 'international sub-contracting' variety. The main basis for such investment is the availability of relatively cheap and easily trainable labour in these countries.[66] All these countries have experienced a rapid rate of growth in their exports of manufactured goods (Appendix Table 5).

Export growth can have far reaching effects on employment. Firstly, there will be the direct effect on employment in the industries engaged in direct production for export. Secondly, there will be the indirect effects on employment in the industries supplying materials and equipment to the export industries. Thirdly, the consumer expenditures of workers employed in all these industries will lead to a further creation of employment. Fourthly, the increased foreign exchange earnings resulting from exports will facilitate importation of equipment and permit increased employment.

All these direct and indirect employment effects of exports have been estimated by Susamu Watanabe for Korea.[67] The direct employment effects of exports were found to be substantially high in the case of finished textile products and textile fabrics. It is instructive to note that nearly 48.4 per cent of clothing exports and 8.3 per cent of textile fabrics were attributable to international sub-contracting. Indirect employment effects on secondary sectors, though present, were not found to be very high. This is a consequence of the heavy reliance by the final goods producers on imported equipment and materials. This is also the reason for the relatively low retained value added in the case of export oriented investments in general. However, Watanabe found evidence of indirect employment effects on the tertiary and services sectors as a result of export led growth. Not surprisingly, Watanabe attributes the success of South Korea in reducing its unemployment rate from 8.1 per cent in 1963 to 4.7 per cent in 1970 to export led growth, much of which is to be attributed to foreign enterprise participation. Singapore has also made impressive strides in employment creation.

What Could Have Been

There is considerable critical speculation on what job opportunities there could have been in the absence of the multinationals. It ranges from the prognosis that the jobs they have created are a mere replacement for previous employment to the belief that they have destroyed rather than created employment opportunities.

---

[66] International sub-contracting is discussed in greater detail in Section E.

[67] S. Watanabe, "Exports and Employment: the case of the Republic of Korea", *International Labour Review*, (December, 1972).

It is possible that in some specific instances multinationals may have merely substituted new jobs for old, albeit at marginally higher wage rates. But as a generalisation this seems implausible in view of the high and rising levels of unemployment in most developing countries. Only a very small proportion of this burgeoning level of unemployent can be accounted for by frictional unemployment.

Even so, could it be that foreign firms have only a limited potential for creating jobs? Is it possible that they have introduced a bias against labour absorption in the developing countries? Could they have moulded local firms in their own image? Behind questions of this sort is the thesis that the techniques of production of the foreign firms are inappropriate to the factor endowments of the developing countries. They are said to be excessively capital-intensive in relation to the labour rich and capital poor developing countries. By introducing excessively capital-intensive techniques into the developing countries, the argument goes, they may have inhibited job creation. To put it simply, their technology is inappropriate.

Inappropriate Technology Thesis

This thesis has five strands — First, it is argued that foreign firms tend to tread the path of least resistance by adopting technologies familiar to them in their home countries. These invariably tend to be capital-intensive. This could be called the 'resistance to change' argument. Second, as they have access to relatively cheap capital in international capital markets and they are often the favoured borrowers in local capital markets also, they are prone to adopt capital-intensive techniques as the most economic. This could be called the 'favoured access to capital' strand of the thesis. Third, they tend to operate in industry groups which by the nature of their operations permit little or no substitution of labour for capital. This could be called the 'technological fixity' strand of the thesis. Fourth, they tend to produce over-packaged, over-specified, and over-differentiated products which contribute to the overall capital-intensity of the production process. This can be called the production-bias strand of the thesis. Fifth, they tend to pay relatively high wage rates for the labour they employ based on international standards. This applies not only for management and skilled labour but also for unskilled labour. This tends to push up the wages rates in the local labour markets, and as a result the local firms are also forced to substitute capital for relatively expensive labour. This could be called the 'contamination of local labour markets' strand of the thesis.

The Evidence

The empirical evidence on most of these issues is mixed. In several instances the operations of foreign firms are shown to be less capital-intensive than that of locally-owned firms. A study on factor proportions in 42 plants in the Kenyan manufacturing sector relating to food processing, textiles, chemicals, paints and plastic containers found the foreign owned firms to be less capital-intensive than locally-owned firms.[68] A similar finding is reported by an ILO employment mission to Kenya.[69] It is of significance that the phenomenon is attributed to the technical perception and managerial expertise of the foreign firms in identifying the existence of labour-intensive techniques rather than to the influence of factor prices. This suggestion brings into doubt the contamination of local labour market's proposition. Not only were the foreign firms less capital-intensive than local firms but their choice of techniques had not been influenced by factor prices. Furthermore, there is enough evidence to show that local firms had the same ease of access to capital as foreign-owned firms. This is reported to be so in Kenya and also in Brazil.[70] This finding challenges the favoured access to capital strand of the thesis also.

The various strands of the 'inappropriate technology' thesis suggest that capital-intensity is in some sense due to the 'foreigness' of foreign firms. Much of the recent empirical evidence suggests, however, that it is not so much the nationality of the firms, as the product market conditions that influence factor proportions. When firms have a monopolistic advantage in product markets they are under less pressure to minimise costs. They tend to tread the path of least resistance and adopt capital-intensive techniques. A novel explanation of this phenomenon runs in terms of the dominance of the 'engineering man' over the 'economic man' in the face of monopolistically oriented product markets.[71] It is argued that in the absence of effective competition in product markets firms tend to push the production process towards advanced automated techniques, the objective of the 'engineering man,' and the 'economic man's' objective of minimising costs takes second place. It is significant that Louis Wells attributes this phenomenon to both locally-owned and foreign-owned firms in his case study on Indonesia.

A prime reason for the presence of highly profitable

[68] Howard J. Pack, "Substitution of Labour for Capital in Kenyan Manufacturing," *Economic Journal*, (March 1976).

[69] ILO, *Employment, Incomes and Inequality*, (Geneva, 1976).

[70] R. S. Morley and G. W. Smith, "Limited Search and Technology Choices of Multinational Firms in Brazil," *Quarterly Journal of Economics*, (May 1977).

[71] Louis T. Wells Jr., "Economic Man and Engineering Man: Choice of Technique in a Low-Wage Country," *Public Policy*, Vol. XXI, (1973).

monopolistically oriented product markets in most developing countries is their pursuit of import-substituting industrialisation policies through the imposition of quotas and tariffs on imports. The permissive market environment this creates encourages the adoption of capital-intensive techniques. A case study of factor proportions adopted by the foreign-owned and locally-owned firms in the Brazilian manufacturing sector attributes the capital-intensity of foreign owned firms to this permissive environment.[72] Such an environment encourages production planners to indulge in satisficing behaviour. In other words, it absolves them from the need to seek out cost minimising techniques, and they tend to adopt techniques of production nearer to their domain of competence. This in fact may be the explanation for the resistance to change strand of the 'inappropriateness' thesis discussed above.

In short, capital intensity cannot be attributed to the 'foreigness' of foreign firms. Local product market conditions may significantly influence their choice of techniques. When product and factor market conditions dictate the adoption of labour-intensive techniques they do not hesitate to do so. Similar evidence is reported in the case of foreign-owned firms in Ghana.[73] Yet another case study of thirteen American-owned firms operating in developing countries concludes that the pressure for adapting production processes rises and falls with the cross elasticity of demand for the product in question.[74] In fact the study suggests that an American firm was more likely to depart from its US technology in low-wage countries if the primary basis was price.

The 'technological fixity' strand of thesis has also not survived empirical tests. Statistical studies both in the developed and developing countries show that sectoral elasticities of substitution between labour and capital are significantly different from zero and range between 0.5 and 1.6.[75] Several studies show that foreign firms have not been slow in seizing opportunities to substitute labour for capital. Such substitution has not only occurred in ancillary activities (handling, packaging, sorting out spares, etc.) but also in the production process itself through adaptation of machinery, greater machine speeds and sub-contracting of production processes.[76]

---

[72] Morley and Smith, *op. cit.*

[73] D. Forsyth and R. Solomon, "Choice of Technology and Nationality of Ownership in Manufcturing in a Developing Country," *Oxford Economic Papers,* (July, 1977).

[74] W. A. Yeoman, *Selection of Production Process for the Manufcturing Subsidiaries of US based Multinational Corporations,* (unpublished DBA thesis, Harvard Business School, April, 1968).

[75] H. J. Bruton, "The Elasticity of Substitution in Developing Countries," Williams College Research Memorandum, No. 45, (Centre for Development Studies, April 1972).

[76] G. K. Boon, "Technological Choice in Metal Working with Special Reference to Mexico," in A. S. Bhalla ed. *Technology and Employment in Industry,* ILO, (Geneva, 1975).

The 'production bias' argument has attracted attention in recent years. There may be something to the argument that foreign-owned firms producing for the domestic market tend to produce over-packaged, over-specified and differentiated products, catering mainly to the upper income groups. This argument, however, raises several issues which await further research. First, do luxury goods necessarily entail capital-intensive methods of production? It is likely that they utilise a relatively high proportion of skilled labour but it is doubtful if they are necessarily capital-intensive. Second, this charge may be valid in the case of final consumer goods. But the proportion of foreign private investment in such goods is unlikely to be high. Third, the production of such goods would respond to a demand for them. Such demand arises because of the highly unequal income distribution prevailing in most developing countries. The solution to the problem would entail correcting income inequalities by fiscal methods. Fourth, if such policies are precluded, the question needs to be asked whether or not it would be wise to allow the production of such goods and impose fairly high purchase taxes on such goods consumed mainly by the rich.

To sum up, the record of the multinationals in job creation is significant though not dramatic. Empirical evidence does not sustain the generalization that foreign-owned firms are *invariably* capital-intensive. In most cases the capital-intensity of foreign firms is not due to their foreignness *per se.* The protected market environment prevailing in most developing countries appears to have influenced their choice of capital-intensive techniques. There is need for re-thinking on the type of incentives and policies the developing countries should adopt to tilt the foreign firms in favour of efficient labour-intensive techniques. This aspect is discussed in the concluding section of this chapter.

E.   THE QUEST FOR CONTROL

Government intervention in international economic relations is nothing new. But the advent of the multinational corporation has introduced new dimensions to international economic diplomacy. No longer is it merely a question of tariff bargaining and market sharing. More weighty issues of political sovereignty and economic independence are involved. And it is not only the developing countries that are concerned about the threat posed to economic sovereignty by the spread of giant corporations with their seemingly unlimited access to technology and resources. In fact, back in 1967, Servan-Schreiber, in his book *The American Challenge,* was merely restating, albeit colourfully and in a European context, the long-felt Canadian and

Australian fears about the spread of American corporations.[77]

The developing countries, however, have been more intense in their concern about foreign enterprise participation in their economies. Perhaps with just cause. Fear of foreign domination of their economies, particularly intense in the case of most developing countries which have shed the yoke of colonialism only recently, is but one of their worries. Much more important is their concern about the share of gains from foreign enterprise participation that accrues to them, which was discussed earlier. They are not so well placed as those countries which are host to foreign private investment in the developed world in exercising 'countervailing power.' They generally lack the expertise and information needed to strike a hard bargain. Their role is confined to playing hosts to foreign firms, unlike many developed countries whose firms interpenetrate each other's markets. Again, while there may be gaps in technology between developed countries, a veritable technological knowledge chasm separates the developed from the developing countries.

It is for these reasons that most developing countries have imposed a web of regulations and restrictions on foreign direct investment. But at the same time, most of them have also been wooing foreign investors with tax concessions. Regulations on FDI can be grouped broadly under two heads:

    a. Restrictions designed to "depackage" the FDI package;
    b. Restrictions on royalty rates and dividend repatriation.

Depackaging

Foreign direct investment, by definition, is a package of capital, technology, marketing and managerial skills. It is often argued that the packaged nature of FDI enables the foreign firms not only to 'overcharge' for the technology they supply to the developing countries but also exercise control over operations. The total returns on the whole combination of capital, technology, marketing and managerial services accruing to the foreign firms may exceed what they could get by selling these ingredients separately.

While the *modus operandi* of foreign firms is often resented, their resources of capital technology and management are eagerly sought. Hence the enthusiasm of developing countries for ways and means by which the FDI package can be 'depackaged'; methods by which capital, technology and managerial skills can be bought separately and assembled together into a successful team by LDCs.

---

[77] For a review of the literature on the reactions of developed countries to MNEs in the early 1970s, see Sperry Lea and Simon Webley, *Multinational Corporations in Developed Countries: A Review of Recent Research and Policy Thinking,* (BNAC, 1973).

The most sought after methods of 'depackaging' are technical collaboration agreements and management contracts. Joint ventures between locally-owned and foreign firms are often recommended to wholly owned foreign subsidiaries.[78] A characteristic feature of these arrangements is the absence of equity ownership in a major way by the foreign firms. It is also the hope that under such arrangements the technology recipient local firms can retain control over operations.

The policy towards prospective foreign enterprise participation in most developing countries is tilted in favour of joint ventures and technical collaboration agreements and against wholly-owned foreign subsidiaries. Furthermore, many developing countries require existing foreign firms to reduce their share of equity holdings in favour of local investors. The intensity of such equity spin-off regulations varies from country to country. Indonesia has recently decreed that all foreign-owned enterprises should reduce their foreign equity to not more than 49 per cent within 10 years.[79] India has also set a deadline before which all foreign-owned enterprises are required to reduce their share of equity holdings to 49 per cent. Only those enterprises which undertake to export a major share of their output are to be exempted from this requirement. Mexico requires that majority ownership should be Mexican in the case of all new enterprises or of expansion of old enterprises into new product lines. The Andean code also required all foreign enterprises taking advantage of the Andean Common Market tariff preferences to agree to spin off their equity to a minority position over a defined period.

Malaysia, Thailand, Brazil and the Philippines have also entry control regulations but of a less restrictive nature. Malaysia requires that all foreign-owned enterprises accept at least 30 per cent Malay participation within five years. Exceptions to this rule are made for enterprises with high labour intensity in their operations and for those exporting a high proportion of their output. 'Pioneer Status' is granted to firms who operate in sectors considered to be 'vital to the public interest.' Tax holidays from two to eight years are accorded to firms which are granted 'pioneer status.' Thailand reserves a number of areas of economic activity to Thai nationals. In other areas the foreign-owned firms are required to limit the growth in their annual production to 30 per cent. Although Thailand has set no time limits on equity dilution, she also favours joint ventures. Brazil has no hard-and-

---

[78] Technical collaboration agreements is a generic term for licensing agreements, technical service agreements and engineering and construction agreements. For definitions and distinctions see V. N. Balasubramanyam, *International Transfer of Technology to India,* (Praeger, New York, 1973). Ch. 2.

[79] For information on regulations, this section draws on Richard S. Robinson, *National Control of Foreign Business Entry: A Survey of Fifteen Countries,* (Praeger, New York, 1976).

fast rules regarding equity spin-off. But it rewards the so-called 'open capital companies,' those that do divest their equity in favour of local nationals, with various forms of tax incentives.

Other Regulations

Most developing countries have imposed regulations on royalty payments and dividend repatriation. For instance, Brazil allows no tax deductions on royalty payments made by subsidiaries to their parents and does not permit capitalisation of intangibles or used capital equipment. Besides, there are stringent controls on technology transfers. Know-how, technical assistance and licensing agreements require approval by the National Institute of Industrial Property. Importers of technology are required to offer justification for the acquisition of technology, provide a summary description of the technology and list the benefits of such technology to the national economy. Most developing countries now also impose ceilings on royalty payments. India, Indonesia, Thailand and Brazil specify an upper limit to royalty rates as a percentage of sales, usually 5 per cent of sales. Mexico and the Andean pact countries also have broadly similar regulations.

Evaluation of the Regulatory Framework

This brief sketch of the main contours of the mechanisms of control over FDI adopted by developing countries shows the diversity of their approach. In most cases the regulatory framework is also exceedingly complex, requiring a high degree of technical and administrative expertise for its implementation. A salient feature of these regulations is that they attempt to guide the behaviour of foreign firms mostly by bureaucratic control. How well conceived are these regulations? And how are the foreign firms responding to them?

As stated earlier most developing countries favour joint ventures and technology licensing agreements and some have decreed that existing foreign firms must 'dilute' their share of equity in favour of local investors. If importation of skills and technology is a prime objective, such regulations may be self defeating. Foreign firms would be reluctant to commit scarce managerial and technical resources to ventures in which they have only a minority interest. The returns they can get from such ventures may not fully compensate them for their investment in the production of knowledge. Furthermore, the absence of functional control over operations of the kind they can exercise through asset ownership may impair their ability to operate efficiently.

Evidence from India suggests that the type of knowledge transferred under technical collaboration agreements was restricted to blueprints, designs and flow charts. Transfers of human skills or more generally corporate skills and capabilities rarely resulted from such arrangements. Although such transfers had occurred in the case of joint ventures they were much less relative to FDI ventures.[80] Again, Richard Robinson reports that most of the twenty managers of foreign subsidiaries he interviewed in Mexico were reluctant to become minority investors in a majority Mexican-owned operation. They were of the opinion that they would not be able to utilise their managerial expertise fully when they had only a minority share in equity. Some observers argue that the slowing of US investment in the Andean Common Market countries is principally due to the restrictions on foreign equity holding laid down in the Decision 24 promulgated in 1970. Given the equity spin-off regulations, the inducement provided by the Andean Code in the form of tariff-free access to the markets of the six-nation Common Market may not have been very effective.

Equity spin-off regulations may also rebound to the disadvantage of host countries in other ways. By manipulating transfer pricing, foreign firms may limit the share of profits accruing to local shareholders and rest content with a minimum return on their investment. Further, if the dividend record of foreign-owned subsidiaries turns out to be poor, its stock may become unattractive and the implementation of equity spin-off that much more difficult. In fact, lack of purchasers for the equity spun off by the foreign firms may itself be a problem for some if not all the developing countries. In the event, the State may have to buy the equity.[81]

The logic of imposing an across-the-board ceiling on royalty rates and dividend repatriation is also questionable. The value of a particular piece of technology is to be determined by the benefits to be derived from it. An overall ceiling may inhibit importation of quality technologies and technology importers may have to resort to other methods of compensating the suppliers.

It is reported that in Brazil the total payment per contract made by foreign subsidiaries was substantially higher than that made by locally-owned firms importing foreign technology. This suggests that foreign subsidiaries had resorted to manipulating transfer pricing as a method of repatriating funds when other avenues were barred.

Again, Indian firms importing technology under licensing agreements reported that more often than not they had to compensate foreign firms in other ways, by paying a premium on imported

---

[80] For details see V. N. Balasubramanyam, *op. cit.,* Ch. 4.

[81] Richard Robinson reports that in the '70s the Mexican stock market remained thin and was a viable route for spinning off equity only for the companies with strong earnings records or those willing to pledge a minimum dividend regardless of profits; Robinson *op. cit.* p 182.

equipment, inspection charges for approving the products and increased commission on sales when the product was exported through the licensor's marketing channels. Furthermore, the executives saw a link between the governments' stipulations on royalties and the restrictions on exports imposed by the licensors. "In regard to governments' insistence on getting export rights, sometimes we find stiff opposition from overseas collaborators. The lump sum amount and the royalty we pay to overseas collaborators for technical collaboration is not found adequate by them for surrendering other markets."[82]

All this is not to suggest that developing countries should exercise no control over inflows of foreign private capital and technology. Some screening might be necessary to discover possible monopolistic practices and importation of technologies which are not in the interests of the country. However, draconian measures stipulating equity spin-offs and restrictions on royalty payments irrespective of the nature of the project may well rebound to the disadvantage of the developing countries imposing them.[83]

Exports and Foreign Enterprise Participation

The new orthodoxy in most developing countries is export-led development. Most developing countries have actively promoted the exports of manufactured goods through the provision of various incentives to both local and foreign firms. As has already been noted several countries exempt export oriented foreign firms from equity spin-off regulations. Indeed, it is the more ebullient hosts to foreign enterprise participation that have achieved a rapid rate of growth in their exports of manufactured goods (Appendix Table 5). The surge in exports achieved by South Korea, Hong Kong, Taiwan, Singapore and Mexico has attracted wide attention in recent years. Their export achievement is largely due to 'international sub-contracting.'

International Sub-contracting

This is an arrangement by which firms in developed countries contract out to producers in the developing countries the manufacture of products, components and processes. The sub-contractor in the developing country may be a wholly owned subsidiary of a foreign firm, a joint venture or a locally owned firm. The foreign entity entering into the contract may be a manufacturing firm or a large

---

[82] V. N. Balasubramanyam, *op. cit.,* pp 89-90.

[83] For a detailed discussion of these issues as applied to FDI in the extractive industries see R. F. Mikesell, *New Patterns of World Mineral Development, op. cit.*

buying house or a departmental store like Boots or Sears Roebuck. The distinguishing feature of such arrangements, however, is that the foreign firm provides the market outlets, know-how, product specifications, designs and in some cases, raw materials.

The availability of relatively inexpensive but easily trainable labour in the developing countries is the main attraction of such arrangements to the firms in the developed countries. For instance, US wages in garment-making were estimated to be 20 times that of South Korea in the year 1967. The net labour costs for electronic assembly in the Far East is estimated to be only 8 per cent of that of the USA.[84] Moreover, differences in labour productivity between the developed and developing countries in most of the assembly type and machine paced operations are negligible. In fact in many industry groups labour productivity may be relatively high in the developing countries. Thus, the increasing tendency on the part of the manufacturing firms in the developed countries to contract out the labour-intensive phases of their production processes to the developing countries.

Apart from production of components and parts for electronics, semi-conductors and various types of machine assembly, international sub-contracting also extends to final goods such as clothing, footwear and toys and games.

Government Policies

The South East Asian countries referred to above are noted for their liberal trade and foreign investment policies. Hong Kong and Singapore have virtually no restrictions on imports of equipment and raw materials. South Korea, though it levies import duties, refunds them to the foreign firms when they have re-exported the materials and equipment in processed form. The Korean Government also provides various subsidies and relief from internal taxes to exporters. In addition, export firms are provided with various overhead facilities. The Massan Free Export Zone provides fully equipped factory sites to both local and foreign firms servicing the export markets. Enterprises in the zone are allowed duty free access to materials and equipment. There are no legal limits on equity participation, although South Korea encourages joint ventures.

Such fiscal incentives to exporters are provided by most of the developing countries. These incentives alone do not adequately explain the relative success of the South East Asian countries referred to earlier in attracting foreign enterprise. More important is the 'climate for

---

[84] M. Sharpston, "International sub-Contracting," *Oxford Economic Papers,* 1974. This article provides a lucid analysis of the economics of international sub-contracting.

foreign investment' prevailing in these countries that explains their success in attracting foreign firms. By 'foreign investment climate' is meant the host country attitudes towards private enterprise, their political stability and the perception of the degree of risks of expropriation felt by the foreign firms.

On all these counts the 'foreign investment climate' prevailing in the four Asian countries could be described as healthy and salubrious. In fact, the surge in foreign investment in Singapore is mainly attributed to these factors and fiscal incentives are reported to have had little effect in attracting foreign firms.[85]

It is sometimes argued that both the growth in foreign enterprise participation and exports of these countries are to be attributed to certain distinct geo-social characteristics they display. They are all relatively small in size and are endowed with a resilient labour force mainly of foreign origin. They may have been forced into exporting because of the small size of their domestic markets. The work discipline and creative characteristics of their labour force are well-known.

This line of reasoning, however, can be carried too far. Relatively small sized domestic markets may push countries towards exporting. But external markets have to be actively sought and promoted. This calls for a high degree of marketing skills and expertise which most developing countries lack. It is to the credit of the four Asian countries that they have overcome this problem by resorting to international sub-contracting. Distinguishing characteristics of this arrangement are that it provides an assured market, and the marketing functions are performed by the foreign firms. In any case, Korea began with an import-substitution strategy and moved towards export-promotion in the 1960s. Again, an endowment of resilient and disciplined work-force could be effectively exploited only if there are market outlets for what they produce. In general, the overriding reason for the export success of the four Asian countries appears to be their political stability and their attitudes towards private enterprise.

It is often argued that export oriented FDI, especially of the international sub-contracting variety, based on the utilisation of cheap labour in the developing countries results in the exploitation of labour.[86] It would amount to exploitation if there were alternative sources of employment for labour in these countries at substantially higher wage rates. But in most of these countries there is substantial

---

[85] See Helen Hughes and You Poh Seng *Foreign Investment and Industrialization in Singapore,* (Australian National University Press, 1969).

[86] Paul Streeten, "The Theory of Development Policy" in J. H. Dunning ed *Economic Analysis and the Multinational Enterprise* (George Allen & Unwin, London, 1974).

urban unemployment and the minimum wage rates offered by foreign firms tend to be well above that required to attract labour, and, indeed may be well above that actually paid in service trade and backyard workshops.[87] In fact a major benefit of export-oriented investment is its job creation potential discussed in a previous section of this chapter. However, many of these countries may have unnecessarily surrendered income to the foreign firms by providing them with capital subsidies and tax incentives: a policy which may have had little impact on the decision of foreign firms to invest in these countries.

International Codes of Conduct

Since the UN Declaration on the New International Economic Order in May 1974, there has been a flurry of activity to formulate codes of conduct on the operations of multinational firms. Several draft codes of conduct already exist and some multinationals themselves have drawn up codes of good behaviour. As yet it is not clear: what form a universally acceptable code of conduct should take, who should enforce it, whether it should be voluntary or mandatory, what should be included and what should be the objectives of the code. Further, the MNEs argue that the codes of conduct should also apply to the host developing countries. They express concern about the danger of appropriation or nationalisation of their assets without adequate compensation. They would like the codes of conduct to reflect their interests also.

Most of the codes that have been formulated bristle with pronouncements to the effect that the multinationals should respect the political sovereignty of the host countries, assist the development efforts of developing countries and support their economic goals and objectives. These are inevitably vague and formulating such codes may turn out to be no more than a cosmetic operation. A code of conduct covering virtually every aspect of the activities of the MNEs such as pricing of technologies, reinvestment of profits, nature of technologies transferred, their spheres of activity etc, would be exceedingly complex and impossible to enforce.

To sum up, most of the developing countries have spun a web of restrictions and regulations on foreign direct investment. The nature and intensity of such regulations differ between countries depending on their economic philosophy and policy objectives. In general, such measures are designed to transfer income from the foreign firms to the

---

[87] Michael Sharpston, *op. cit.,* p 102.

host countries. Although there is a case for regulating foreign enterprise participation, some countries appear to have over-extended themselves in this direction by measures that are not only conflicting, but sometimes also self-defeating. The more ebullient hosts, mostly in South East Asia have pursued a relatively liberal policy towards foreign direct investment. This has significantly contributed to the strides they have made in exports and employment. It is however, to be recognised that the impressive growth performance of these countries is also to be attributed to their political stability, the political emphasis that these countries place on exporting, their attitude towards private enterprise and the climate for foreign private investment they provide. As such, though their experience with export led growth has lessons for other countries, it may not signal a universal recipe for development.

Statistical Appendix to Chapter III

INDEX

Appendix Table 1

Parent Enterprise Concentration of Foreign Direct Investment

Home Country	Stock of Foreign Direct Investment 1971 ($ billion)	Concentration			
		Year	Number of Trans- national Enterprises	Per cent of Foreign Direct Investment Accounted for	Amount of 1971 Stock of Foreign Investment Accounted for by Specified Number of Enterprises ($ billion)
United States	$86.0	1966	50	55%	$47.3
United Kingdom	24.0	1962	52	71	17.1
Federal Republic of Germany	7.3	1964	24	52	3.9
Switzerland	6.8	1965	7	65	4.4
Canada	5.9	1963	13	70	4.2
Japan	4.5	1972	20	28	1.3
Sweden	3.5	1965	5	50	1.7
TOTAL of above countries	138.0		171	58	79.9
World	165.0	1969-1970	over 10,000	100	165.0

Source: Karl P. Sauvant, "The Potential of Multinational Enterprises as Vehicles for the Transmission of Business Culture," in Karl P. Sauvant and Farid G. Lavipour (eds), *Controlling Multinational Enterprises: Problems, Strategies, Counterstrategies* (Boulder: Westview Press, 1976).

Appendix Table 2

Sectoral Distribution of Stock of Private Investment in the Developing Regions, 1972

	Africa		Latin America & Carribean		Asia and Oceania		Middle East		All Developing Countries	
	$ billion	%	$ billion	%	$ billion	%	$ billion	%	$ billion	%
Petroleum	4.1	45.0	5.3	23.5	2.4	29.6	3.6	87.8	15.4	35.0
Manufacturing	1.6	17.5	8.9	39.4	2.5	30.8	0.3	7.3	13.3	30.3
Mining	1.5	16.5	2.2	9.7	0.6	7.4	—	—	4.3	9.8
Others	1.9	21.0	6.2	27.4	2.6	32.2	0.2	4.9	10.9	24.9
TOTAL all sectors	9.1	100.0	22.6	100.0	8.1	100.0	4.1	100.0	43.9	100.0

Source: *Transnational Corporations in World Development* (UN, New York, 1978), p 260.

Appendix Table 3

Sectoral Distribution of Accumulated US Foreign Direct Investment in the Developing Countries 1966, 1970, 1975 and 1978 (year-end values and percentage distribution)

	1966	1970	1975	1978
TOTAL ($ billion)	$16.2	$25.0	$34.9	$40.5
Petroleum	45.9%	39.9%	32.0%	11.2%
Manufacturing	24.1	22.0	30.0	34.8
Mining	11.4	10.1	6.2	5.8
Services	14.2	*	25.0	39.5
Others	8.1	28.1	6.8	8.8

Sources: 1966: *Survey of Current Business,* Vol. 48, No. 10, October 1968.
1970: *Survey of Current Business,* Vol. 53, No. 9, September 1973.
1975: *Survey of Current Business,* Vol. 56, No. 8. August 1976.
1978: *Survey of Current Business,* Vol. 59, No. 8, August 1979.
* "Services" is included in "Others" in 1970.

Appendix Table 4

Stock of Foreign Direct Investment in Selected Countries of Asia ($ million)

	1967	1972	1976
Hong Kong	$65	$400	$1,480
South Korea	18	300	1,150
Malaysia	103	300	2,400
Singapore	40	150	1,330
Taiwan	88	500	1,670

Source: For 1967 and 1972: *The Impact of Multinational Enterprises on Employment and Training* (ILO, Geneva, 1976).
1976 figures from *Development Co-operation DAC 1978 Review* (OECD, Paris, 1978).

Appendix Table 5

Pattern and Growth of Exports: Selected Developing Countries

	Value of Manufactured Exports (1969) Million $	Manufacturing Exports as % of Total Exports (1969)	Annual Average Growth Rate of Total Exports % (1965-70)	Annual Average Growth Rate of Exports of Manufactures % (1962-69)	Approximate Share of Multinationals in Exports of Manufactures % (1972)
Hong Kong	$1,484	67.4%	17.1%	20.1%	10.0%
Taiwan	570	57.0	26.0	36.5	20.0
South Korea	365	60.8	36.7	77.1	15.0
Malaysia	130	8.1	6.5	18.0	n.a.
Brazil	244	10.6	11.4	16.2	43.0
Mexico	380	27.0	4.5	19.8	25–30
Philippines	138	15.3	6.8	10.2	n.a.
India	547	30.0	3.0	6.1	5.0
Indonesia	20	2.8	7.6	21.3	n.a.

Source: UNCTAD, Trade in Manufactures of Developing Countries. Various Annual reports.

IV. Summary and Conclusions

Each of the issues treated in this study — Aid, Short-term Finance and Foreign Direct Investment — generates areas of controversy and of conflict between the developing countries and the developed industrial nations. But there are also areas of common ground where progress, though not easy, should be possible. We have tried to identify such points of mutuality and to make at least tentative suggestions for ways of helping LDCs without damaging the interests of the DCs.

CHAPTER I: AID

In the past, donor nations have stressed the benevolent nature of their programmes of assistance to LDCs yet the statistical evidence suggests that foreign policy and commercial objectives have dominated in motivating the distribution of bilateral ODA. Also, arguments used to justify overseas aid to their own legislatures and voters have stressed advantages to their own nations from the provision of ODA. Such motivation does not form a sound basis for the promotion of development and runs a serious risk of backfiring on donors, as LDCs resent such economic imperialism.

ODA is also relatively small, less than 8 per cent of the total capital available to LDCs. Its actual value is further reduced by interest and repayment conditions, by source tying and by project tying. Hence it is not surprising that it has proved difficult to demonstrate much positive effect on overall economic and social progress in LDCs. But there is a broad consensus that increasing the rate of investment in physical and human capital (or trained people) is an important determinant of increased growth. ODA can be a significant contributor to both, and in some nations has been a major factor, e.g. Malawi and Kenya.

If ODA could be separated from short run political and commercial objectives it could become more relevant to the task of raising living standards in LDCs. Expanding the proportion which goes through multilateral channels is one way by which this could be done.

The small volume of ODA is well below agreed UN targets of 0.7 per cent of GNP in most donor nations. The immediate prospects of increasing it through unorthodox means such as taxes on fishing, seabed mineral extraction or emigrants from LDCs are not good, but in the longer run are worth exploring. However, if more assistance is to be provided for development through financial transfers from rich to poor countries, the main line for progress may be improvements in the quality rather than the quantity of aid. This would require a reduction in aid tying, an increase in the amounts passing through multilateral channels and an enlargement of the grant element, all of which represent ways in which ODA could provide more development per dollar expended. However, such changes would risk reducing the amount of ODA as interest groups, such as exporting firms in some donor DCs, would have less to gain from untied aid and would cease to lobby for ODA. Whether this would occur sufficiently to offset the gain from improved quality of ODA is a matter of judgement with little to base it on save that a few countries notably Sweden, Norway and the Netherlands, have simultaneously increased, multilateralised and improved the terms of their ODA. On the other hand, Canada's new administration is threatening to reverse recent liberal trends in its international aid.

From the viewpoint of the LDCs, improvements in the quality and quantity of ODA are clearly desirable, but it is not immediately apparent they are in the interests of the DCs. At the present time there may be a case that expansion of untied ODA from those OECD and OPEC countries with balance of payments surpluses could help to reduce the recession by stimulating demand, but the same objective could be obtained by domestic expansion. Normally any increase in ODA implies an opportunity cost in terms of reduced consumption or investment at home in order to transfer resources abroad. Aid tying does not avoid that cost, it merely reduces it by raising the price of the goods supplied. Those who strongly support increased ODA can only hope that a moral imperative will prevail or, what is much the same thing that a belief in a very long-run enlightened self interest will lead DCs to improve both the quality and the quantity of aid.

CHAPTER II: DEBT, FINANCE AND THE INTERNATIONAL MONETARY SYSTEM

Most countries must be able to borrow money in order to meet emergencies. Some, including middle income nations such as Brazil, Mexico and South Korea, can borrow from world financial markets through bank loans, bond issues and suppliers' credits. But most of the poor LDCs (per capita incomes under $400 in 1978) lack a sufficiently high credit rating and find it difficult to borrow commercially at reasonable terms. As a result, the problem of servicing a large commercial debt is centered on a few relatively prosperous LDCs. Up to 1978 they appear to have been able to handle the problem, assisted by growing exports and a rate of world inflation which lowered the real costs of debt. They even added to their reserves. But, after the revolution in Iran with its effect on oil prices and the damage to world trade, some middle income LDCs may well run into difficulties in meeting their debt obligations while covering their current account deficits.

The more successful ones should be able to maintain their credit lines and roll over loans, but some may falter. Some of the commercial banks in the rich nations may feel over-exposed in foreign loans or may come under pressure from conservative monetary authorities. This is likely to mean that the commercial banks will be less able to channel OPEC and OECD surpluses to LDCs than they did in 1974-77. At the very least this is a credible risk. To avoid the serious consequences of any breakdown of international confidence, there is a need to provide medium term official finance to those countries which, for no fault of their own, seem at risk of default or serious hardship. The IMF's Supplementary Financing Facility is one way of doing this. But it needs more resources and its three year maximum lending rule may have to be relaxed. The conditions imposed by the IMF should strengthen investors' confidence and may make it easier for a country which follows them to obtain supplementary bank loans. Such strengthening of international finance would be in the interests of all nations.

For most of the poorer LDCs the main financial problem is shortage of long term loans and grants. Often they do not have many projects which can show quick or high commercial returns and they cannot afford to repay loans quickly or meet high interest payments. Softer ODA is the key to this problem. But the poorer LDCs also have liquidity problems even though the sums involved are relatively small. Bunching of repayments of past loans, unforeseen drops in exports and surges in import bills for oil or food are the main causes. Since they are seldom able to borrow much from banks they are dependent on official finance. In principle, increases in their existing quotas in the Fund and access to the IMF Compensatory Financing Facility (CFF) can be the main solution to their balance of payments difficulties. But the CFF needs to be improved, particularly to take better account of export trends, to recognize fluctuations in exports of services and changes in the price of imports.

Improvements in the efficiency with which the international monetary system can cope with temporary payments imbalances are evidently in the interests of all. Clearly DCs and LDCs should work together to achieve such improvements when the threat to world prosperity arising from the huge OPEC surpluses is apparent. The solution of the liquidity and adjustment issues are paramount. Besides these the 'Link' objective is minor. Nevertheless although the net gains to LDCs from a link between aid and the creation of SDRs may be small, it is particularly worthwhile during a recession. Thus, for the DCs to concede it could be a worthwhile indication of goodwill towards LDCs.

CHAPTER III: FOREIGN DIRECT INVESTMENT AND INTERNATIONAL TRANSFER OF TECHNOLOGY

This chapter has analysed the major issues relating to private foreign direct investment (FDI) in the manufacturing sectors of the developing countries. In the main these issues relate to the sharing of the rewards from FDI between the multinational enterprises (MNEs) and the developing countries, the implications of FDI for employment and the regulations imposed by developing countries on the multinationals.

Sharing of Rewards

Because of the small number involved, FDI does contribute an element of 'monopoly' to the profits of many MNEs, which is augmented by the protectionist policies pursued by several developing countries. However, the frequently argued thesis that the profits made by MNEs *ipso facto* amount to exploitation of the developing countries is an exaggeration.

The exploitation thesis is based on a misconception of the nature of the market for techology and a misinterpretation of the theory that knowledge is a free good. Knowledge is regarded as a free good in the sense that the marginal cost of replicating existing knowledge is zero. But this line of reasoning ignores the fixed costs of R and D involved in its production, the costs of transferring technology and the need to preserve the incentives for the continued production of knowledge.

The spread between the marginal costs of producing knowledge and the full costs of producing it is quite wide. It is highly unlikely that the actual price charged would be at one extreme or the other. The price, in practice, settles somewhere in the middle. The lower limit would be the one below which the foreign firms would find it uneconomic to stay in the R and D business and the upper limit is determined by the strength of the demand for such knowledge.

It is possible that in several cases, the developing countries may be paying more than the necessary minimum price for technology because they lack information and bargaining strength. Official policy in these countries should, therefore, concentrate on providing information to local firms on alternative sources and streams of technology and the payments to be made for them. The latter objective may not be served by imposing overall ceilings on royalty rates and technology fee payments. This may drive out the 'good' along with the 'bad' suppliers of technology. The need is for information and not bureaucratic interference.

Misuse of Transfer Pricing

Much public attention is paid to the misuse of transfer pricing by MNEs, and to methods of mitigating such practices. There is little information on the extent of such misuse, although some MNEs are known to engage in this practice as a method of maximising the returns to their investment. The principal motivation for the practice, however, appears to arise from the ceilings imposed by the host countries on repatriation of profits, royalty rates and technical fees.

The suggested solutions to the problem mainly boil down to recommending checking prices of imported equipment and comparing them with 'arm's length' prices. This could be done by pooling information on the customs evaluation of imported goods by various countries and disseminating such information. But the scope for this may be limited. There may be no comparability between the types of equipment imported by firms operating in different countries. In many cases comparable 'arm's length' prices do not exist. In the final analysis, there may be no alternative to removing the incentives for certain transfer pricing practices. It may be in the interests of developing countries to relax restrictions on remittances and regulation of royalty rates and tighten their fiscal surveillance.

Indeed, the developing countries may have much to gain by co-ordinating their tax policies. It is doubtful if the various tax concessions, tax holidays, capital subsidies and generous depreciation allowances offered by many developing countries have had an appreciable impact on the inflow of foreign private capital. Such competitive tax concessions may have resulted merely in the developing countries surrendering income to the foreign firms. At the very least the developing countries could agree on a common code of taxation designed to check the loss of tax revenues arising from indiscriminate tax policies.

Employment Aspects

A frequent criticism of foreign direct investment is that the technologies that accompany it are inappropriate to the factor endowments of the developing countries, and that it often inhibits rather than creates employment opportunities. But the record of the MNEs in the sphere of job creation has been quite impressive, particularly in the case of export oriented economies such as South Korea and Singapore. Even the experience of Brazil and Mexico shows that the multinationals have contributed to the overall growth of employment.

Although the operations of foreign firms do tend to be relatively capital intensive, it cannot be argued that they are invariably so; their capital-intensity cannot be attributed to their 'foreigness' *per se*. There are cases where the operations of the foreign firms have been much more labour intensive than that of comparable local firms. They have also not been slow in seizing opportunities for substituting labour for capital.

More often than not their capital-intensity is to be ascribed to the protected product market environment prevailing in the developing countries. The import substitution strategy of many of the developing countries has provided monopolistic markets to both foreign and local firms. In the absence of competitive pressures the foreign firms have opted to employ capital-intensive techniques which are nearer to their domain of competence. In many cases, locally owned firms have also followed suit. The policy producing the most economic benefit in these cases would be to increase the degree of competition in the product markets This can be achieved by the pursuit of liberal trade and investment policies and in general an 'outward looking' programme of development. The complicated entry regulation systems imposed by many of the developing countries on foreign investment may have served only to enhance the monopolistic advantages in product markets enjoyed by the existing firms. Moreover, developing countries would be well advised to subsidise the employment of labour rather than capital. Some developing countries like Malaysia do offer incentives to foreign firms which operate with labour intensive technologies.

However, it may be injudicious to promote labour intensive technologies as an end in itself. The need in most LDCs is for rising incomes and rising employment and not employment at any cost. Increased tax revenues from the operations of foreign-owned firms could be utilised to create jobs elsewhere in the economy. But if in each and every case foreign-owned firms are enjoined to maximise employment it may undermine their efficiency and actually reduce the tax revenues accruing to the government, not to mention discouraging future expansion of MNEs.

Regulations of Developing Countries

A number of developing countries now require foreign firms to 'spin off' all their equity in favour of domestic nationals and to aceept either a minority or a joint-venture status. Many countries waive this regulation if foreign firms are export oriented. This regulation has the dual objective of reducing foreign control over operations and transferring income from the foreign firms to the host countries. Few would quarrel with the objectives of this policy, but its success in attaining these objectives is doubtful. In many cases such a policy may amount to 'killing the goose that lays the golden egg.' Foreign firms may be loath to surrender managerial control and in the absence of such control they may be unable to do what they are equipped to do: transmit technology and skills and minimise costs of production.

Beyond this there is always the possibility that foreign firms would resort to other methods of transferring income when they are denied the conventional channel of dividend repatriation. Use of transfer pricing is one example, and the charging of higher rates of royalty and technical fees in the case of joint ventures is another. The ensuing loss of tax revenues may be too high a price to pay for the benefit of local ownership of equity.

Such equity spin-off and joint venture regulations may succeed only in cases where the host country and the local partners have something substantial to offer the foreign firms. These may be local raw material resources, specific skills or knowledge of local markets. Possession of such advantages is likely to be rare in the case of most manufacturing enterprises, as opposed to mineral ventures, especially if the product is destined for export. A judicious policy option may lie in allowing majority ownership of equity to foreign firms (51 per cent) and instituting effective tax policies to transfer income from the foreign firms. While restrictions and regulations may serve other goals, they are likely to deprive the developing countries not only of their share of income arising out of the operations of foreign firms but also of technology.

For much the same reasons, others methods of unbundling the foreign investment package such as technical collaboration agreements may be of doubtful validity. On grounds of cost considerations alone there appears to be little to choose between foreign direct investment and other methods of importing capital and technology. These other methods are also unlikely to ensure effective control over operations by the local firms. And operationally they are also relatively poor conduits of technology.

All this is not to say that developing countries should dispense with all other methods of foreign enterprise participation in favour of wholly owned subsidiaries. The relative costs and benefits of the various options should be weighed and where appropriate they should initiate joint ventures and technical collaboration agreements. But it should be recognised that the scope for such alternatives may be limited. Beyond that the preconditions necessary for their success must must be recognised. The main precondition is the need to improve the technology absorptive capacity of local firms. This would require a major re-direction of the science and education policies of developing countries towards adaptive rather than basic research. This again is an area where State action is needed not only in funding such research but in establishing links between commercial enterprises and research institutions.

Although most developing countries are striving at attain these preconditions, they lack the resources to achieve a speedy transformation. In any case the building up of a technological infrastruture is characterised by long gestation lags. It may be judicious to recruit the assistance of foreign subsidiaries in building up such an infrastructure. This could be done by encouraging sub-contracting arrangements between foreign owned firms and local firms and subsidising labour training and employment in foreign firms.

Thus, while in principle there may be a case for equity spin-off, fade out arrangements and unbundling, these could only be implemented gradually by attaining the pre-conditions necessary for their success, not be setting pre-determined deadlines and *force majeure*.

Codes of Conduct

Perhaps the most conspicuous efforts to provide some regulatory framework for MNEs are in the establishment by a number of international organisations of codes of conduct covering different aspects of MNE activity. While these are theoretically useful, the sheer variety and complexity of FDI suggests that they will have little chance of being an effective means of curbing what some LDCs see as undesirable practices.

In the final analysis, the task of utilising FDI to serve the interests of development rests as much on the developing countries as it does on the multinationals. The central task facing the policy-maker is how best to harness the acknowledged prowess of the MNE as an agent of change without at the same time undermining its very capability to do so. That FDI is mutually beneficial to the foreign firms and the developing counrties ought to be recognised, and distrust and confrontation should yield to negotiation and understanding.

Members of the British-North American Committee

DONALD M. COX
Director and Senior Vice President
Exxon Corporation, New York, N.Y.

FRANK J. CUMMISKEY
IBM Vice President and President,
General Business Group/International IBM
Corporation, White Plains, New York

JAMES W. DAVANT
Chairman of the Board and Chief Executive
Officer,
Paine Webber Incorporated, New York, N.Y.

DIRK DE BRUYNE
Managing Director,
Royal Dutch/Shell Group of Companies,
London

WILLIAM DODGE
Ottawa, Ontario

WILLIAM H. DONALDSON
Dean,
Yale School of Organization and
Management, New Haven, Connecticut

*PETER DONIS
Executive Vice President,
Caterpillar Tractor Company, Peoria, Illinois

GEOFFREY DRAIN
General Secretary,
National Association of Local Government
Officers, London

JOHN DU CANE
Chairman and Managing Director,
Selection Trust Limited, London

DONALD V. EARNSHAW
Senior Staff Executive,
Continental Can Company, Stamford,
Connecticut

GERRY EASTWOOD
General Secretary,
Association of Patternmakers and Allied
Craftsmen, London

HARRY E. EKBLOM
Chairman and Chief Executive Officer,
European American Bancorp, New York, N.Y.

MOSS EVANS
General Secretary,
Transport and General Workers' Union,
London

J. K. FINLAYSON
Vice Chairman,
The Royal Bank of Canada, Montreal, Quebec

GLENN FLATEN
First Vice President,
Canadian Federation of Agriculture, Regina,
Saskatchewan

ROBERT M. FOWLER
Chairman, Executive Committee.
C. D. Howe Research Institute, Montreal,
Quebec

GWAIN H. GILLESPIE
Senior Vice President-Finance,
Heublein Inc., Farmington, Connecticut

MALCOLM GLENN
Executive Vice President,
Reed Holdings Inc., London

GEORGE GOYDER
British Secretary, BNAC
Long Melford, Suffolk

JOHN H. HALE
Executive Vice President,
Alcan Aluminium Limited, Montreal, Quebec

THE HON. HENRY HANKEY
Director, Lloyds Bank International Ltd.,
London

AUGUSTIN, S. HART, JR.
Vice Chairman,
Quaker Oats Company, Chicago, Illinois

FRED L. HARTLEY
Chairman of the Board and President,
Union Oil Company of California, Los
Angeles, California

G. R. HEFFERNAN
President,
Co-Steel International Ltd., Whitby, Ontario

HENRY J. HEINZ II
Chairman of the Board,
H. J. Heinz Company, Pittsburgh,
Pennsylvania

ROBERT HENDERSON
Chairman, Kleinwort Benson Ltd., London

HENDRIK S. HOUTHAKKER
Professor of Economics,
Harvard University, Cambridge, Massachusetts

TOM JACKSON
General Secretary,
Union of Post Office Workers, Clapham,
London

DONALD P. JACOBS
Dean, Graduate School of Management,
Northwestern University, Evanston, Illinois

---

* Became a member of the Committee after the statement was circulated for signature.

JOHN V. JAMES
Chairman of the Board, President and Chief Executive Officer,
Dresser Industries Inc., Dallas, Texas

GEORGE S. JOHNSTON
President,
Scudder, Stevens & Clark, New York, N.Y.

JOSEPH D. KEENAN
President,
Union Label and Services Trades Department, AFL-CIO, Washington, D.C.

TOM KILLEFER
Chairman of the Board and Chief Executive Officer,
United States Trust Company of New York, N.Y.

CURTIS M. KLAERNER
President and Chief Operating Officer,
Commonwealth Oil Refining Company,
San Antonio, Texas

H.U.A. LAMBERT
Chairman,
Barclays Bank International Ltd., London

HERBERT H. LANK
Honorary Director,
Du Pont Canada Inc., Montreal, Quebec

WILLIAM A. LIFFERS
Vice Chairman,
American Cyanamid Company, Wayne,
New Jersey

RAY W. MACDONALD
Honorary Chairman,
Burroughs Corporation, Stuart, Florida

CARGILL MacMILLAN, JR.
Senior Vice President,
Cargill Inc. Minneapolis, Minnesota

J. P. MANN
Vice Chairman,
United Biscuits (Holdings) Ltd., Isleworth, Middlesex

WILLIAM A. MARQUARD
Chairman, President and Chief Executive Officer
American Standard Inc., New York, N.Y.

A. B. MARSHALL
Chairman, Bestobell Ltd., Slough, Bucks.

DENNIS McDERMOTT
President,
Canadian Labour Congress, Ottawa, Ontario

WILLIAM J. McDONOUGH
Chairman, Asset & Liability Management Committee,
The First National Bank of Chicago, Chicago, Illinois

WILLIAM C. Y. McGREGOR
International Vice President
Brotherhood of Railway, Airline & Steamship Clerks, Montreal, Quebec

DONALD E. MEADS
Chairman and President,
Carver Associates, Plymouth Meeting, Pennysylvania

PATRICK M. MEANEY
Group Managing Director,
Thomas Tilling Limited, London

C. J. MEDBERRY III
Chairman of the Board,
BankAmerica Corporation & Bank of America NT & SA, Los Angeles, California

SIR PETER MENZIES
Welwyn, Herts

JOHN MILLER
Vice Chairman,
National Planning Association, Washington, D.C.

DEREK F. MITCHELL
Chairman and Chief Executive Officer,
BP Canada Limited, Montreal, Quebec

JOSEPH, P. MONGE
Chief Executive Officer,
California Life Corporation, Los Angeles, California

DONALD R. MONTGOMERY
Secretary-Treasurer,
Canadian Labour Congress, Ottawa, Ontario

ALLEN E. MURRAY
President of Marketing and Refining Division,
Mobil Oil Corporation, New York, N.Y.

KENNETH D. NADEN
President,
National Council of Farmer Cooperatives, Washington, D.C.

WILLIAM S. OGDEN
Executive Vice President,
The Chase Manhattan Bank, N.A., New York, N.Y.

PAUL PARE
President and Chief Executive Officer,
Imasco Ltd., Montreal, Quebec

PAUL L. PARKER
Executive Vice President,
General Mills Inc., Minneapolis, Minnesota

FRANK A. PETITO
Advisory Director,
Morgan Stanley & Co. Incorporated, New York, N.Y.

BROUGHTON PIPKIN
Chairman, BICC Limited, London

GEORGE J. POULIN
General Vice President,
International Association of Machinists & Aerospace Workers, Washington, D.C.

SIR RICHARD POWELL
Hill Samuel Group Ltd., London

ALFRED POWIS
Chairman and President,
Noranda Mines Limited, Toronto, Ontario

J. G. PRENTICE
Chairman of the Board,
Canadian Forest Products Ltd, Vancouver, British Columbia

LOUIS PUTZE
Consultant, Rockwell International, Pittsburgh Pennsylvania

CARL E. REICHARDT
President and Director,
Wells Fargo Bank, San Francisco, California

BEN ROBERTS
Professor of Industrial Relations,
London School of Economics, London

HAROLD B. ROSE
Group Economic Advisor,
Barclays Bank Limited, London

DAVID SAINSBURY
Director of Finance,
J. Sainsbury Ltd., London

WILLIAM SALOMON
Limited Partner,
Salomon Brothers, New York, N.Y.

A. C. I. SAMUEL
Handcross, Sussex.

NATHANIEL SAMUELS
Vice Chairman,
Kuhn Loeb Lehman Brothers International,
Chairman,
Louis Dreyfus Holding Company Inc.,
New York, N.Y.

SIR FRANCIS SANDILANDS
Chairman,
Commercial Union Assurance Company Ltd, London

HON. MAURICE SAUVE
Executive Vice President, Administrative and Public Affairs,
Consolidated-Bathurst Inc., Montreal, Quebec

PETER F. SCOTT
President,
Provincial Insurance Company Ltd., Kendal, Westmoreland

ROBERT C. SEAMANS, JR.
Massachusetts Institute of Technology, Cambridge, Massachusetts.

LORD SEEBOHM
A Director,
Finance for Industry, London

THE EARL OF SELKIRK
President,
Royal Central Asian Society, London

JACOB SHEINKMAN
Secretary-Treasurer,
Amalgamated Clothing & Textile Workers' Union, New York, N.Y.

LORD SHERFIELD
Chairman,
Raytheon Europe International Company, London

R. MICHAEL SHIELDS
Managing Director,
Associated Newspapers Group Ltd., London

GEORGE L. SHINN
Chairman,
The First Boston Corporation, New York, N.Y.

WILLIAM E. SIMON
Blyth, Eastman, Paine, Webber,
New York, N.Y.

GORDON R. SIMPSON
Chairman,
General Accident Fire and Life Assurance Corporation Ltd., Perth, Scotland

SIR ROY SISSON
Chairman,
Smiths Industries Limited, London

ARTHUR J. R. SMITH
President,
National Planning Association, Washington, D.C.

*SIR LESLIE SMITH
Chairman, BOC International, London.

---

* Became a member of the Committee after the statement was circulated for signature.

Sponsoring Organizations

The British-North American Research Association was inaugurated in December 1969. Its primary purpose is to sponsor research on British-North American economic relations in association with the British-North American Committee. Publications of the British-North American Research Association as well as publications of the British North American Committee are available at the Association's office, 1 Gough Square, London EC4A 3DE (Tel. 01-353 6371). The Association is recognized as a charity and is governed by a Council under the chairmanship of Sir Richard Dobson.

The National Planning Association is a private, nonpolitical organization, founded in 1934, that carries on research and policy formulation in the public interest. NPA was founded during the great depression of the 1930s, when conflicts among the major economic groups — business, farmers, labour — threatened to paralyze national decision making on the critical issues confronting American society. It was dedicated, in the words of its statement of purpose, to "getting [these] diverse groups to work together . . . to narrow areas of controversy and broaden areas of agreement . . . [and] to provide on specific problems concrete programs for action planned in the best traditions of a functioning democracy." NPA is committed to the view that the survival of a functioning American democracy under the increasingly rigorous conditions of the 20th century requires not only more effective government policies but also preservation of private economic initiative and the continuous development by the major private groups themselves of a consensus on how to cope with the problems confronting the nation at home and abroad.

NPA works through policy committees of influential and knowledgeable leaders from business, labour, agriculture, and the professions that make recommendations for dealing with domestic and international developments affecting the well-being of the United States. The research and writing for these committees are provided by NPA's professional staff and, as required, by outside experts. In addition, NPA's professional staff undertakes a wide variety of technical research activities designed to provide data and ideas for policy makers and planners in government and the private sector. These activities include the preparation on a regular basis of economic and demographic projections for the national economy, regions, states, and metropolitan areas, and counties; policy-oriented research on national goals and priorities, employment, manpower needs and skills, health, energy, environment, science and technology, and other economic and social problems confronting American society; and analyses and forecasts of changing international realities and their implications for U.S. policies.

NPA publications, including those of the British-North American Committee, can be obtained from the Association's office, 1606 New Hampshire Avenue, N.W., Washington, D.C. 20009 (Tel. 202-265-7685).

The C.D. Howe Research Institute is a private, nonpolitical, nonprofit organization founded in January 1973, by the merger of the C.D. Howe Memorial Foundation and the Private Planning Association of Canada (PPAC), to undertake research into Canadian economic policy issues, especially in the areas of international policy and major government programs.

HRI continues the activities of the PPAC. These include the work of three established committees, composed of agricultural, business, educational, labour, and professional leaders. The committees are the Canadian Economic Policy Committee, which has been concentrating on Canadian economic issues, especially in the area of trade, since 1961; the Canadian-American Committee, which has dealt with relations between Canada and the United States since 1957 and is jointly sponsored by HRI and the National Planning Association in Washington; and the British-North American Committee. Each of the committees meets twice a year to consider important current issues and to sponsor and review studies that contribute to better understanding of such issues.

In addition to taking over the publications of the three PPAC committees, HRI releases the work of its staff, and occasionally of outside authors, in four other publications: *Observations*, six or seven of which are published each year; *Policy Review and Outlook*, published annually; *Special Studies*, to provide detailed analysis of major policy issues for publication on an occasional basis; and *Commentaries*, to give wide circulation to the views on issues of current Canadian interest.

HRI publications, including those of the British-North American Committee, are available from the Institute's offices, suite 2064, 1155, Metcalf Street, Montreal, Quebec H3B 2X7 (Tel. 514-879-1254).